James R. Murray

Royal Praise for the Sunday School

A Collection of New and Selected Gospel Songs

James R. Murray

Royal Praise for the Sunday School
A Collection of New and Selected Gospel Songs

ISBN/EAN: 9783337162856

Printed in Europe, USA, Canada, Australia, Japan

Cover: Foto ©Lupo / pixelio.de

More available books at **www.hansebooks.com**

FOR THE

SUNDAY SCHOOL.

— A —

COLLECTION OF NEW AND SELECTED

GOSPEL*SONGS,

WITH A CLEAR AND CONCISE COURSE OF INSTRUCTION
IN THE ELEMENTS OF MUSIC.

— BY —

J. R. MURRAY.

CINCINNATI :
Published by The JOHN CHURCH CO., 74 W. Fourth St.,

CHICAGO:
ROOT & SONS MUSIC CO.,
200 Wabash Ave.

NEW YORK:
THE J. CHURCH CO.,
19 East 16th Street.

PUBLISHERS' PREFACE.

The Publishers of Royal Praise believe it to be a worthy addition to their well-known and widely-used series of books for the Sunday-school.

It is not only a new collection, but a collection of new songs, only a few "old favorites" being reprinted.

The Author has given special attention to the words of the book, and a careful examination will show them to be healthy and helpful in sentiment and happily expressed.

The Elements of Music and Course of Practical Exercises will be of value not only to the young, but to all who wish to learn to read by note.

We take pleasure in presenting Royal Praise to the Sunday-schools of America, believing that it will receive from them a hearty welcome.

The John Church Co.

Copyright, 1888, by The John Church Co.

Royal Praise

Royal Praise.

J. R. M.   J. R. MURRAY.

1. Roy-al Praise come let us sing To our Sav-ior, Lord and King. For the love that crowns our days Let us give him Roy-al Praise, Let us give him Roy-al Praise.
2. Roy-al Praise to him be giv'n, Who is Lord of earth and heav'n. O let men and an-gels raise To Je-ho-vah Roy-al Praise, To Je-ho-vah Roy-al Praise.
3. Roy-al Praise to him a-lone Who re-deemed us for his own, Lead-ing us in heaven-ly ways, O to him be Roy-al Praise. O to him be Roy-al Praise.

Copyright, 1888, by the JOHN CHURCH Co

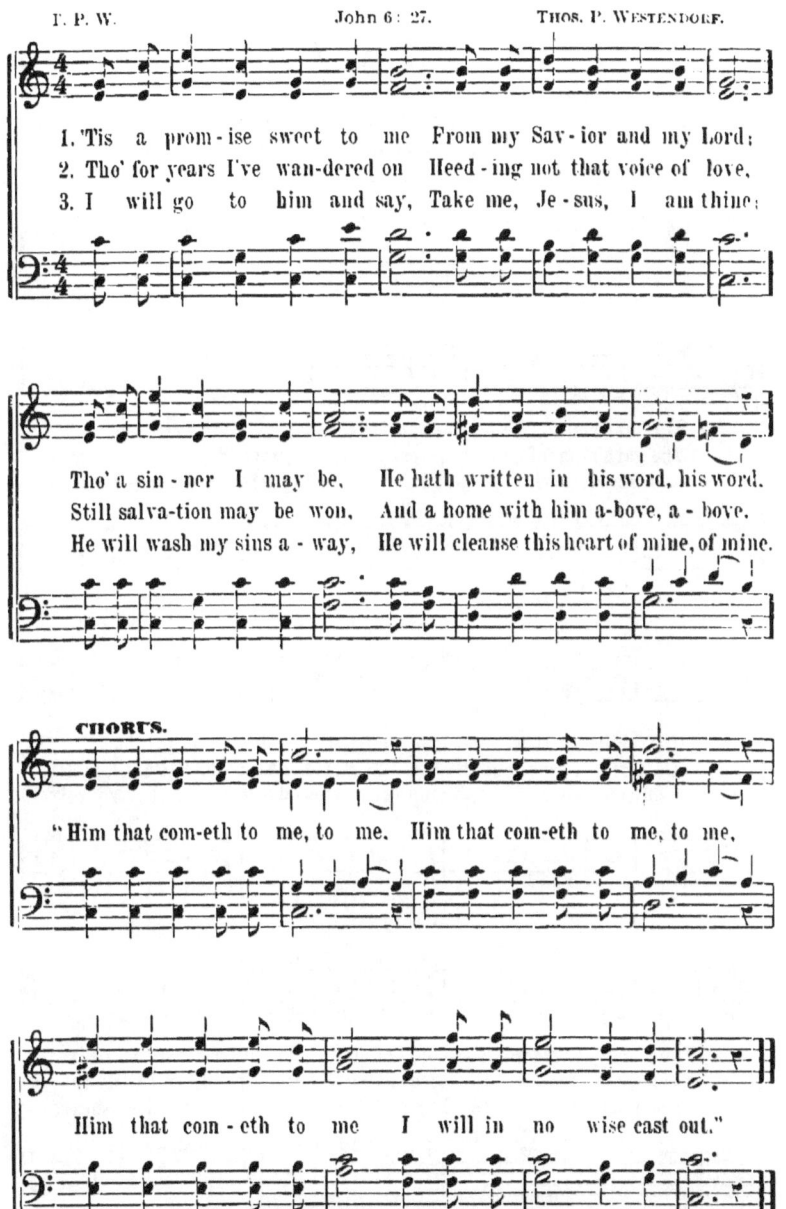

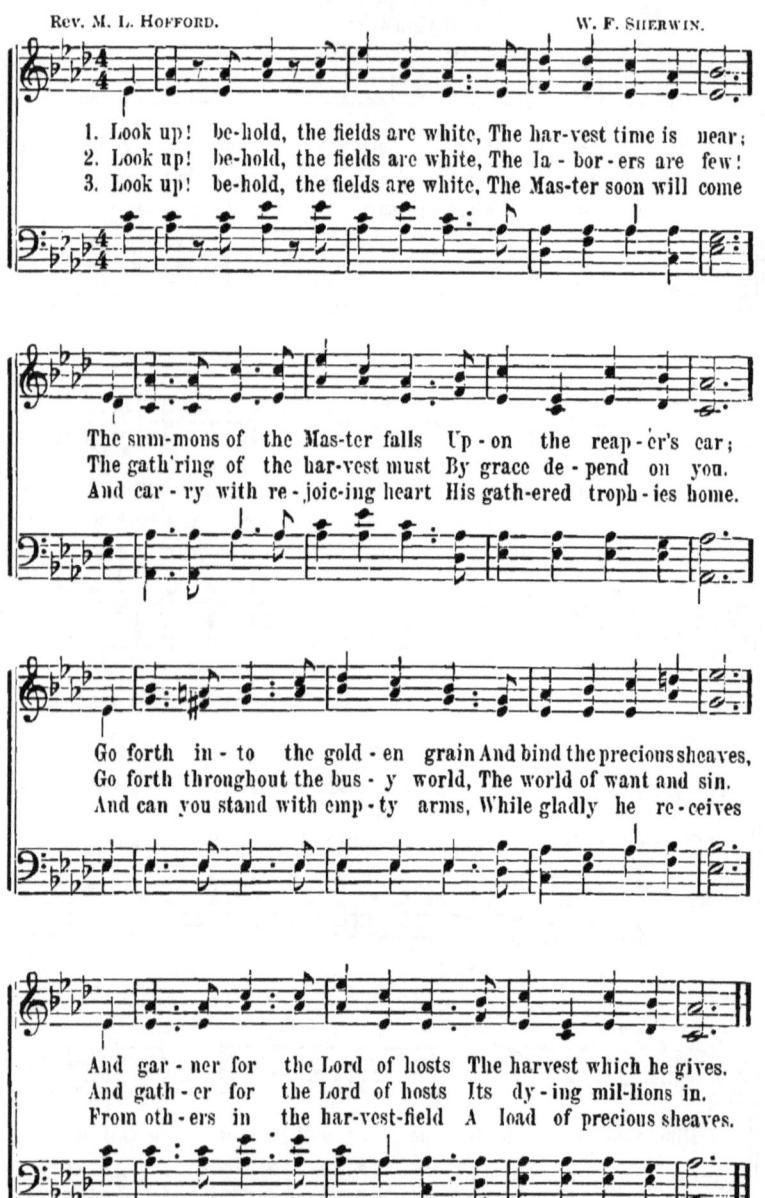

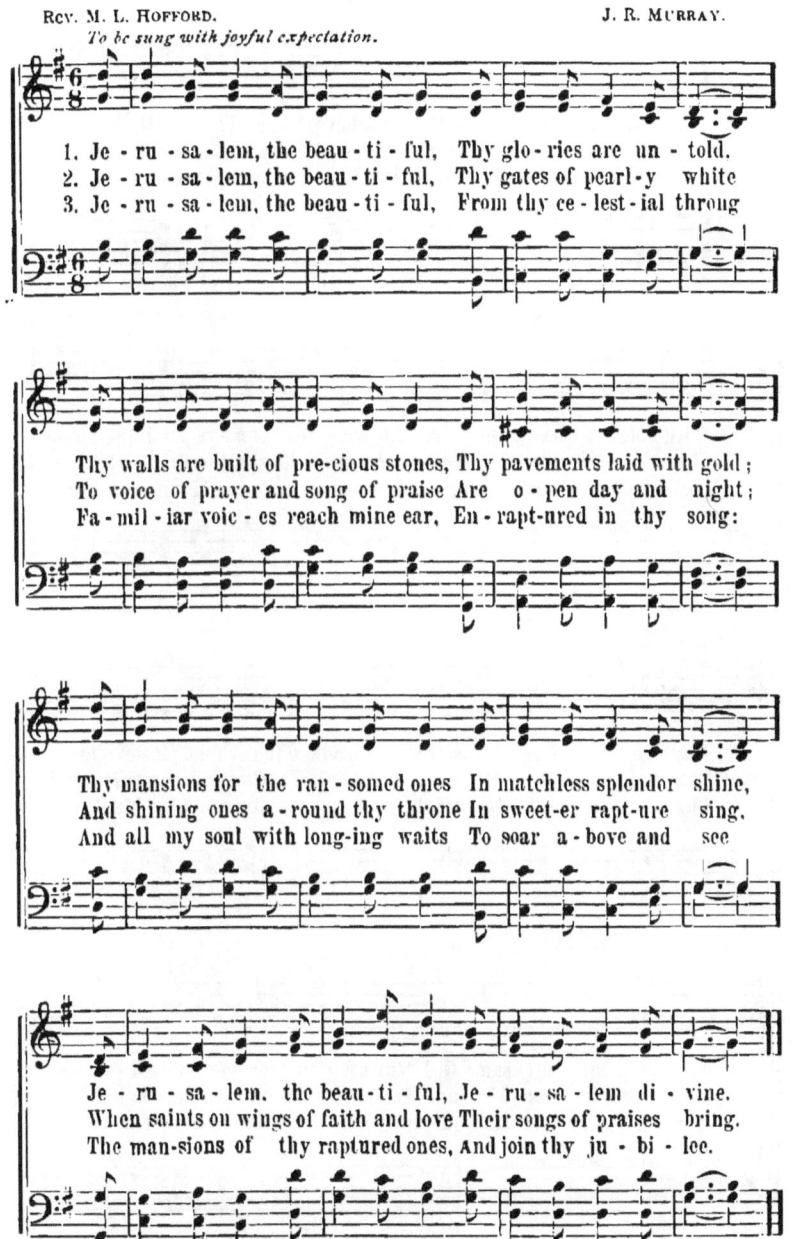

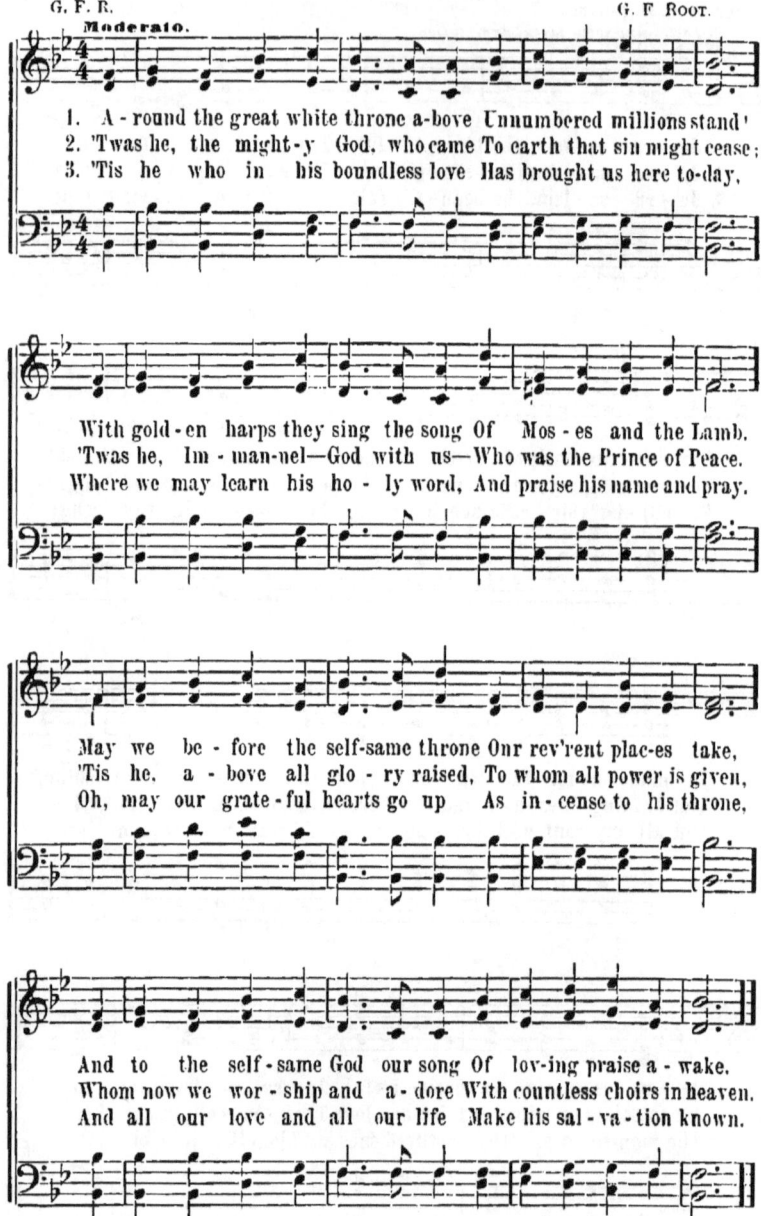

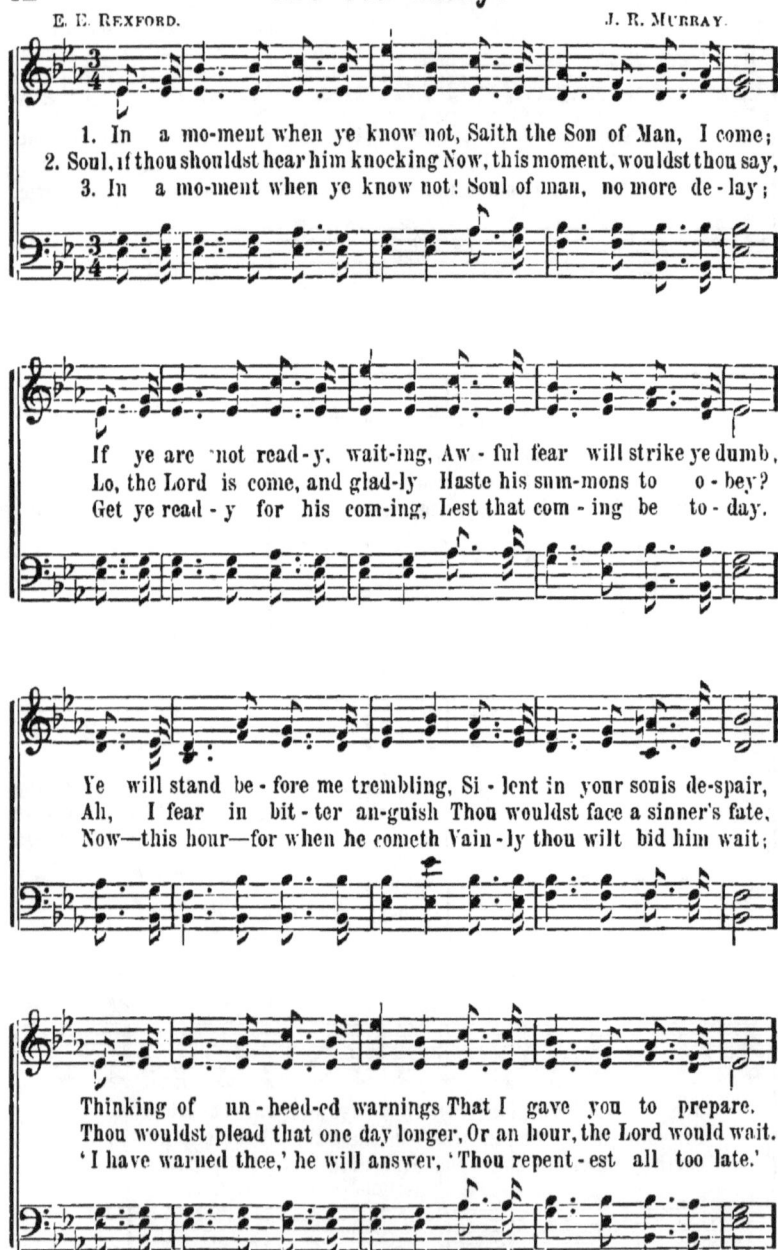

Are You Ready?

13

CHORUS.

Are ye read-y? are ye read-y? O my soul, de-lay no more;
Get ye read-y for his com-ing Ere the Lord is at thy door.

Something each Day.

G. F. R., by per.

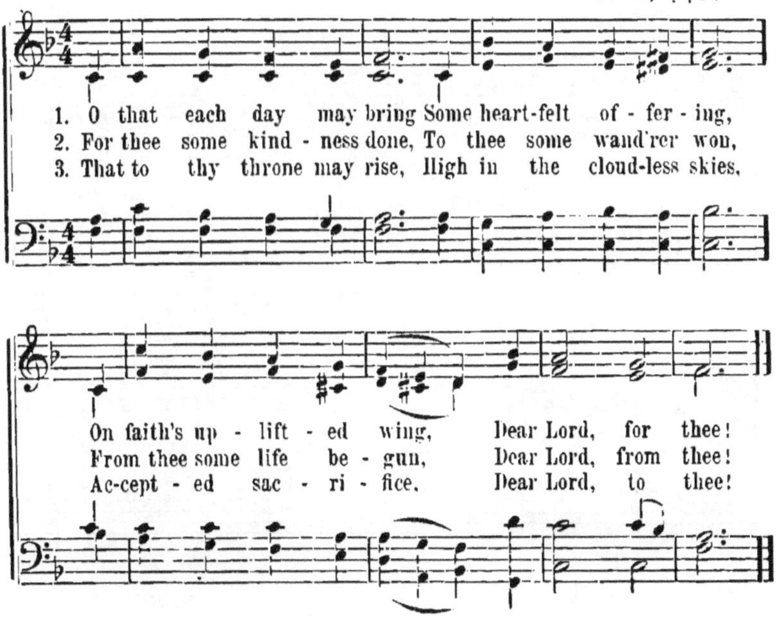

1. O that each day may bring Some heart-felt of-fer-ing,
2. For thee some kind-ness done, To thee some wand'rer won,
3. That to thy throne may rise, High in the cloud-less skies,

On faith's up-lift-ed wing, Dear Lord, for thee!
From thee some life be-gun, Dear Lord, from thee!
Ac-cept-ed sac-ri-fice, Dear Lord, to thee!

14. Our Risen Lord.

EMMA PITT.   JOHN R. SWENEY, by per.

1. We come with sweetest an-thems To greet our ris-en Lord!
2. And we with heart-felt prais-es For hopes that can not die
3. Out from the lone-ly pris-on Im-mor-tal hopes a-rise;

What theme in earth and heav-en Can pur-er joy af-ford?
Would come to join our voic-es In praise to Christ on high.
The por-tals now that o-pen Lead us to Par-a-dise.

CHORUS.

Sing glo - - ry, praise and hon-or To Je - - sus,
Sing glo-ry, glo-ry praise and hon-or To Je-sus, to Je-sus,

King of kings, With angel hosts triumphant. The same sweet music rings.

Thou Hast Called Me.

15

Rev. E. A. Hoffman. J. H. Tenney, by per.

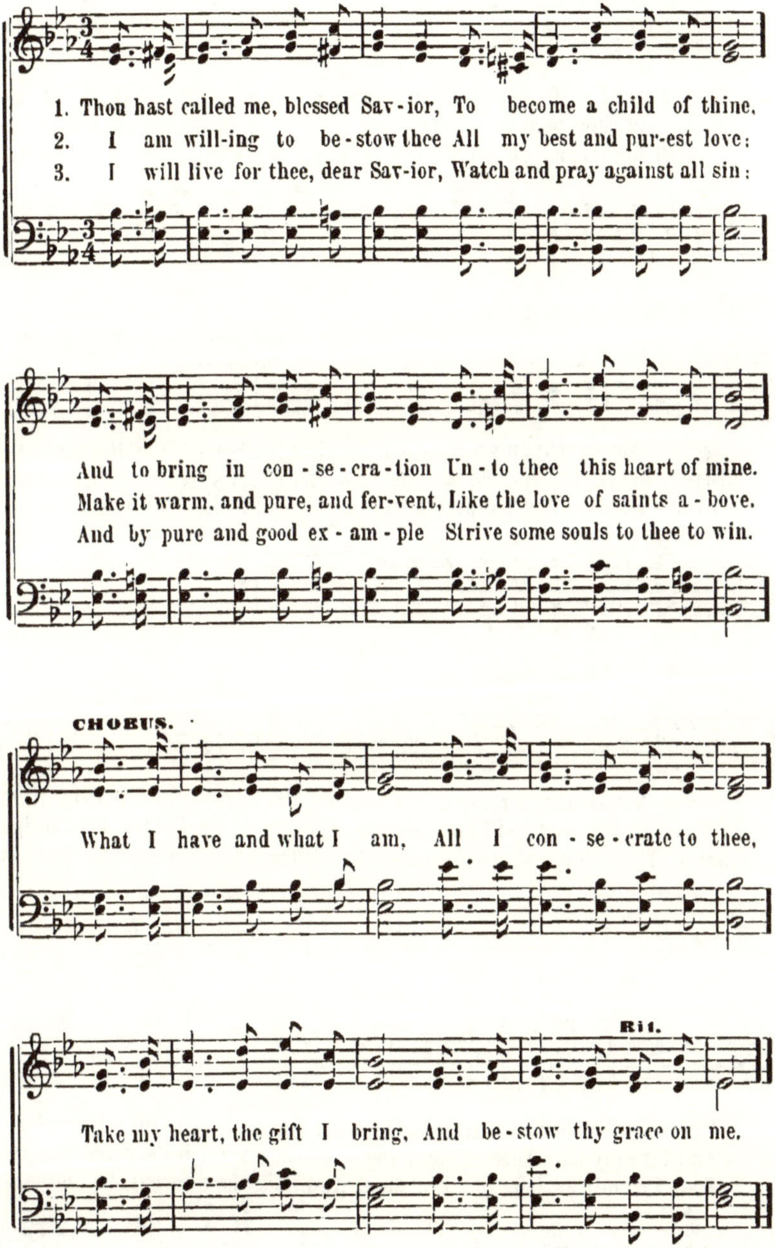

1. Thou hast called me, blessed Sav-ior, To become a child of thine,
2. I am will-ing to be-stow thee All my best and pur-est love;
3. I will live for thee, dear Sav-ior, Watch and pray against all sin;

And to bring in con-se-cra-tion Un-to thee this heart of mine.
Make it warm, and pure, and fer-vent, Like the love of saints a-bove.
And by pure and good ex-am-ple Strive some souls to thee to win.

CHORUS.

What I have and what I am, All I con-se-crate to thee,

Rit.

Take my heart, the gift I bring, And be-stow thy grace on me.

16. Not Worthy, But Willing.

J. R. M.

1. Not worthy, O Lord! of thy par-don, Not fit to partake of thy
2. It is not because I have asked thee, Tho' thou hast encouraged my
3. Still higher, as on-ward I jour-ney, My will ris-es up tow'rd thine

grace; Not worthy, my Savior, but longing To live in the light of thy
prayer; But thou, who dost love me, hast offered My sins and my sorrows to
own; For God has accepted a sin-ner, And I have been giv-en a

face. Not worthy to cling to thy promise Of cleansing and healing divine.
bear. God offered and I have accepted The cleansing, the joy, and the light,
throne. There never was soul so unworthy To meet with compassion like thine,

But ea-ger to come at thy bidding, And claim all thou givest as mine.
And into my life there is flow-ing, A wonder-ful beauty and might.
That I should be heir to a kingdom, And God, the e-ternal, be mine.

Copyright, 1887, by THE JOHN CHURCH CO.

Have You not a Word for Jesus? 19

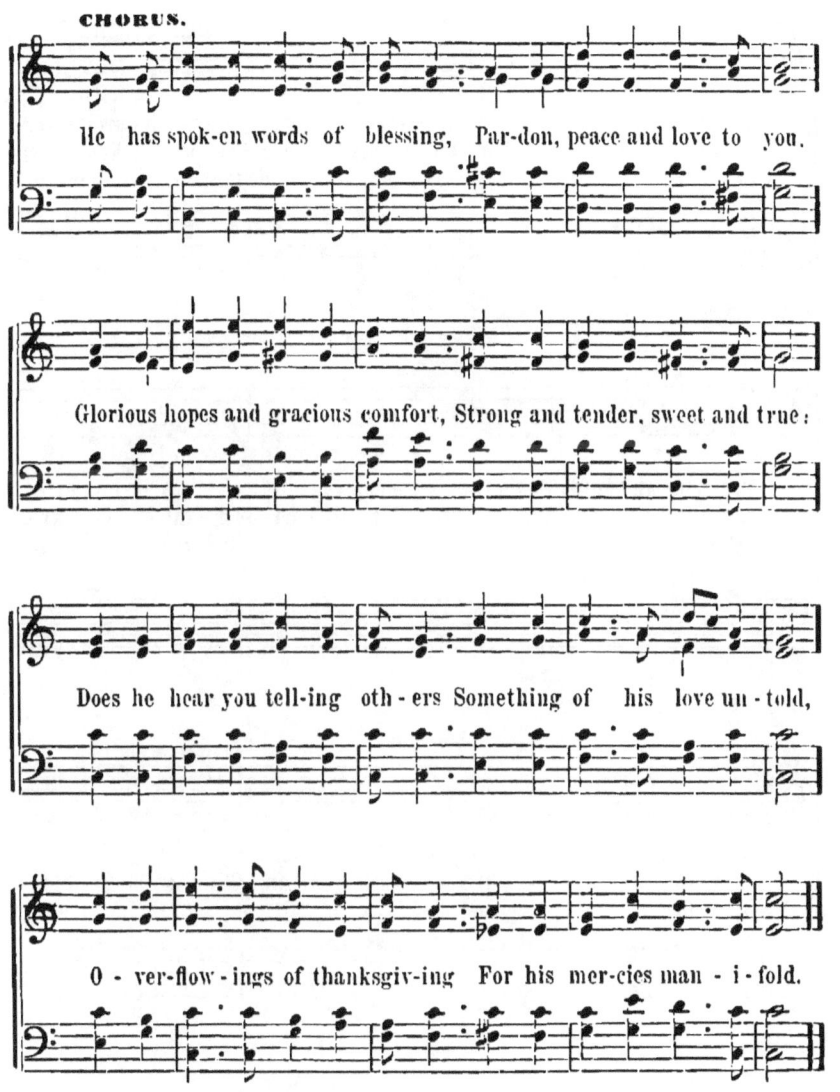

4 Yours may be the joy and honor
  His redeemed ones to bring.
Jewels for the coronation
  Of your coming Lord and King.
Will you cast away the gladness
  Thus your Master's joy to share,
All because a word for Jesus
  Seems too much for you to dare?

Cling to the Bible.

M. J. Smith. J. R. Murray.

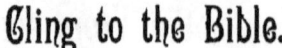

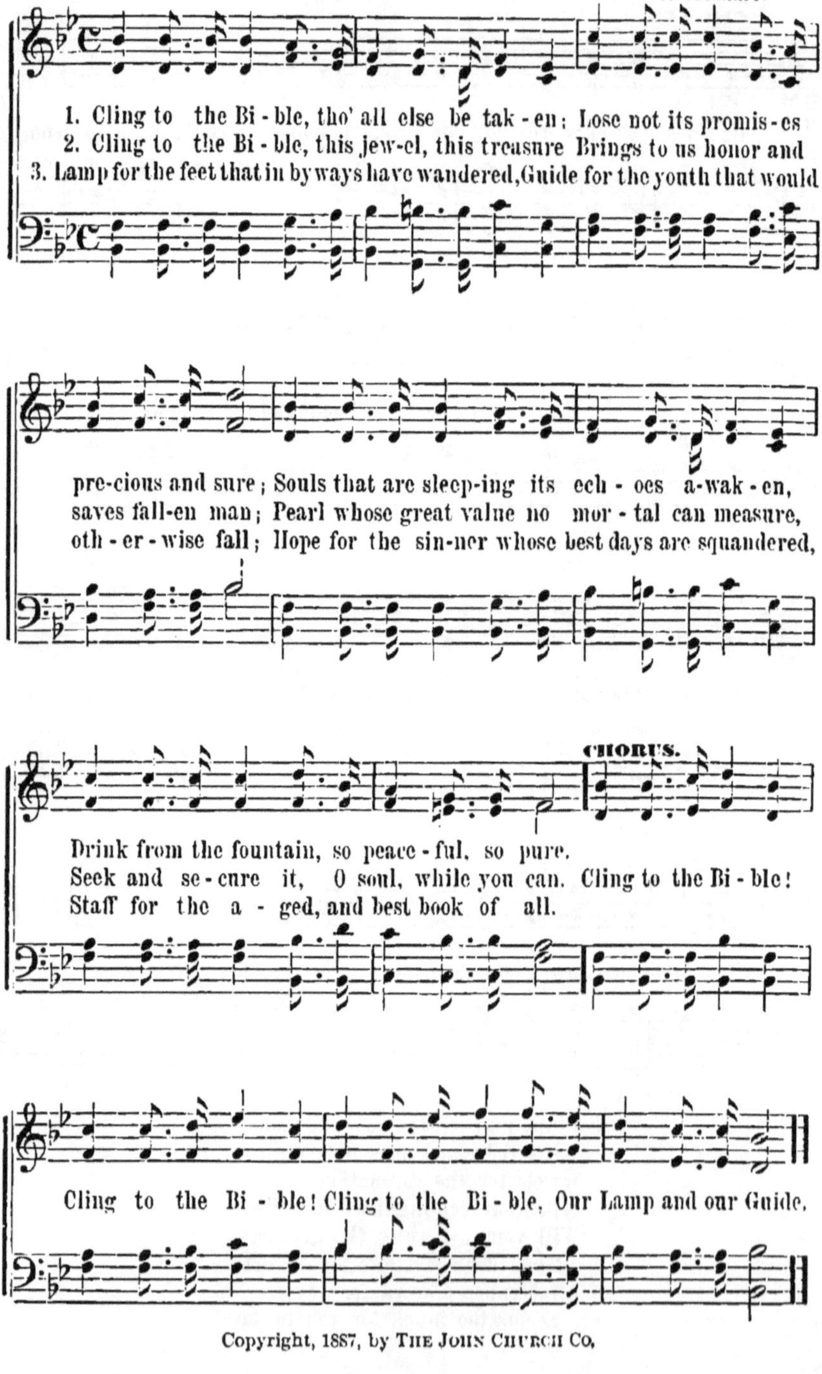

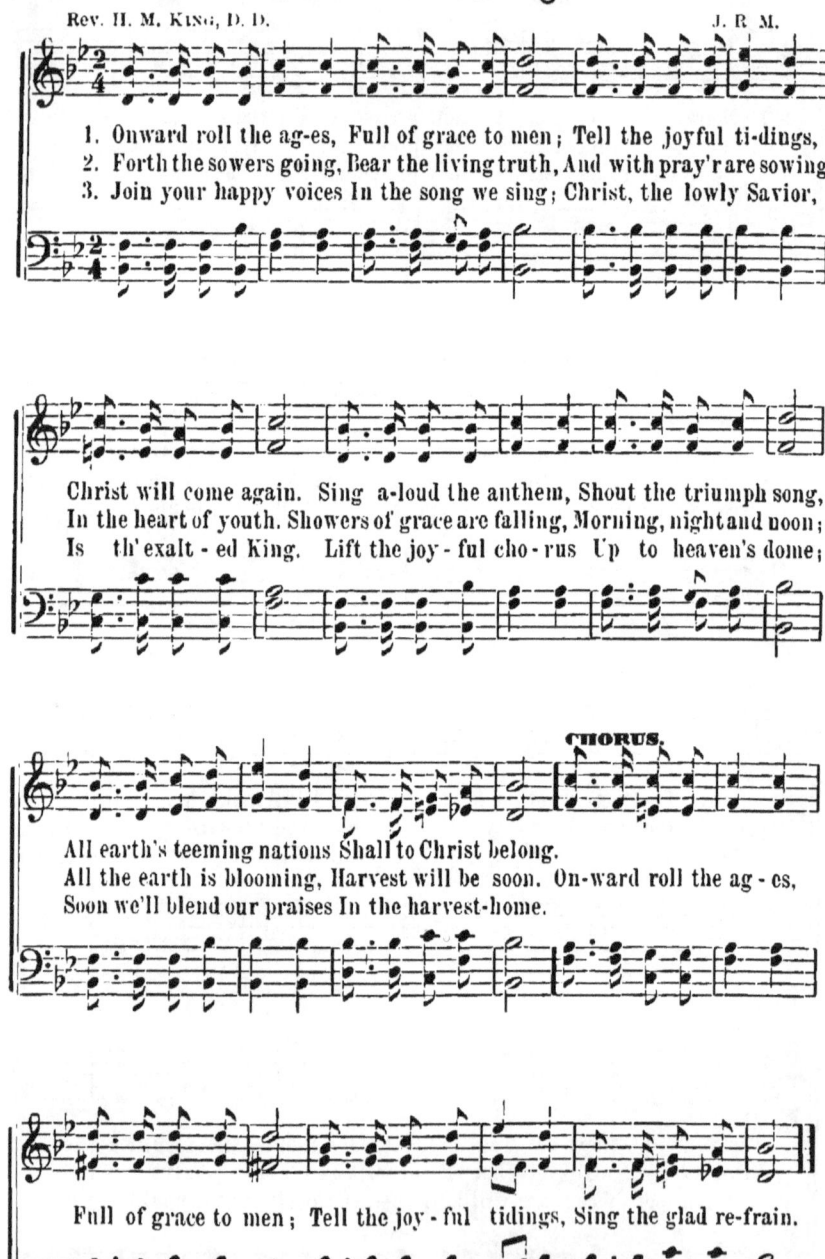

Children's Hosanna. 23

JOSHUA KING. 1819.

1. When his sal - va - tion bringing, To Zi - on Je - sus came,
2. And since the Lord re - tain - eth His love to chil-dren still,
3. For should we fail pro-claiming Our great Re-deem-er's praise,

Cho.—Fling out, fling out the ban-ner Of Christ our heav'nly King;

Fine.

The chil-dren all stood sing-ing Ho - san - na to his name.
Tho' now as King he reigneth On Zi - on's heav'n-ly hill.
The stones our si - lence shaming, Would their ho - san - nas raise.

Ring out, ring out Ho - san - na, And Hal - le - lu - jah sing.

Nor did their zeal of - fend him, But as he rode a - long,
We'll flock a - round his ban - ner, We'll bow be-fore his throne,
But shall we on - ly ren - der The trib-ute of our words?

D. C. Chorus.

He let them still at - tend him, And smiled to hear their song.
And cry a - loud, Ho - san - na To Da - vid's roy - al Son.
No; while our hearts are ten - der, They too shall be the Lord's.

24. Come, O Mighty Savior.

"Where two or three are gathered together in my name there am I in the midst of them."—Matt. 18: 20.

Words and music by G. F. R.

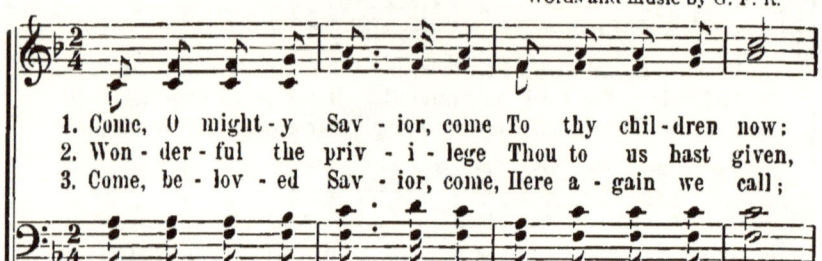

1. Come, O might-y Sav-ior, come To thy chil-dren now;
2. Won-der-ful the priv-i-lege Thou to us hast given,
3. Come, be-lov-ed Sav-ior, come, Here a-gain we call;

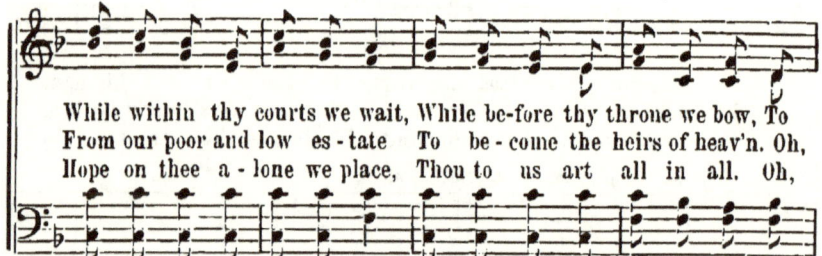

While within thy courts we wait, While be-fore thy throne we bow, To
From our poor and low es-tate To be-come the heirs of heav'n. Oh,
Hope on thee a-lone we place, Thou to us art all in all. Oh,

ev-'ry bur-dened heart draw near, Near each an-xious soul,
help us by thy might-y power From these bonds to soar,
turn some soul from er-ror's ways Ere the hour is flown,

Let thy hand of love and power Touch and make them whole.
Clothed in thine own right-eous-ness, Sons for ev-er-more.
Bring some way-worn wand-'rer back To his Fa-ther's home.

Copyright, 1888, by The John Church Co.

26 Go, Preach my Gospel.

ALICE M. SCHOFF. J. R. M.

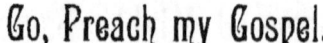

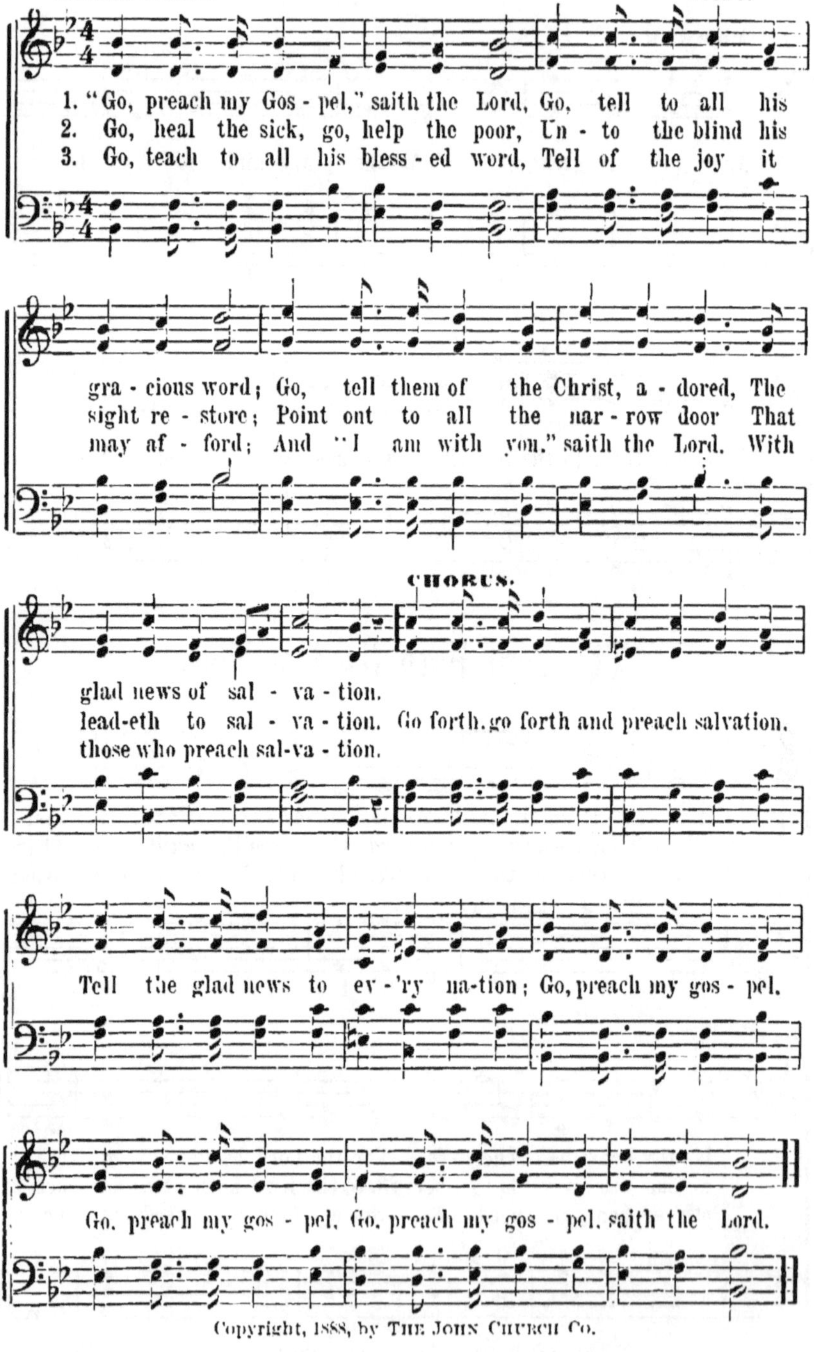

3 Others have sown where you now may reap,
   Though they have gone to their long, long sleep,
   Jesus his promises all will keep,
     Behold now the harvest time.
   Now is the joy of the fallen race,
   Now is the fulness of gospel grace,
   Now does the Master reveal his face,
     Now is the harvest time.

Rich in Mercy.

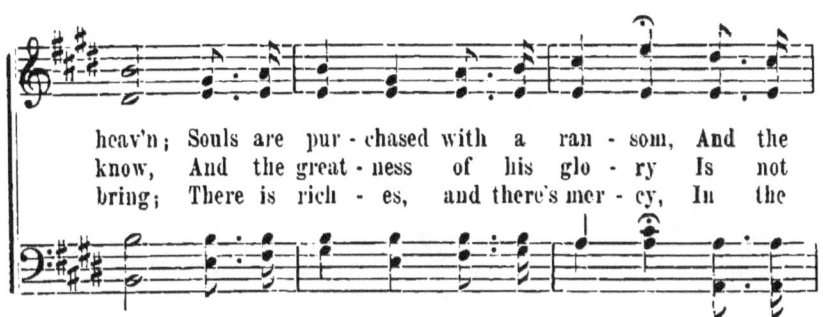

The Lord Will Hold thy Hand.

31

"I, the Lord, * * * * will hold thy hand." Isa. 42: 6.

Rev. J. S. B.   Rev. J. S. Boyd.

1. In help-less guilt I lay, un - til I heard love's sweet command.
2. Then pardoned, saved, and wholly cured, I sought a like-blest band.
3. A pil - grim still, I'm trav-el - ing To Canaan's hap - py land;
4. O soul, if doubts becloud thy faith, Still on the prom - ise stand;

"A - rise and walk to do my will; The Lord will hold thy hand."
In lov - ing work grew more assured, The Lord will hold my hand.
My guid-ing star I see, and sing, The Lord doth hold my hand.
Hear what the voice from heaven saith, "The Lord will hold thy hand."

CHORUS.

The Lord will hold thy hand, O yes, The Lord will hold thy hand; What-

Ad lib.

e'er be - tid - ing, Safe homeward guiding, The Lord will hold thy hand.

Copyright, 1888, by THE JOHN CHURCH CO.

32. Are You Coming?

T. P. W.
Thos. P. Westendorf.

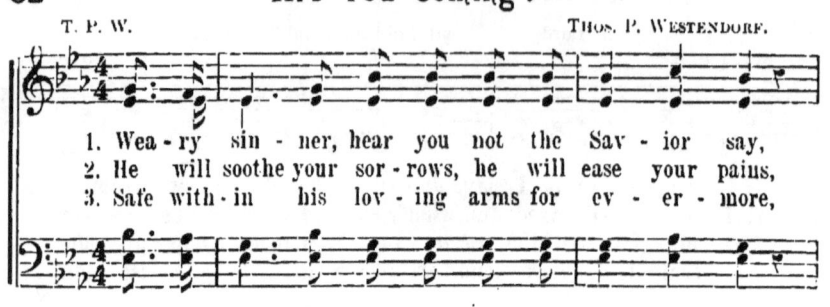

1. Wea-ry sin-ner, hear you not the Sav-ior say,
2. He will soothe your sor-rows, he will ease your pains,
3. Safe with-in his lov-ing arms for ev-er-more,

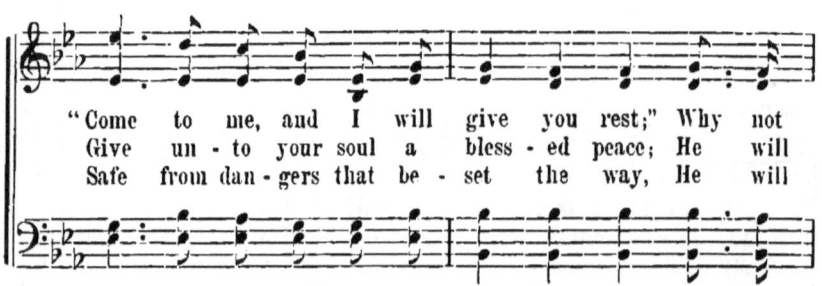

"Come to me, and I will give you rest;" Why not
Give un-to your soul a bless-ed peace; He will
Safe from dan-gers that be-set the way, He will

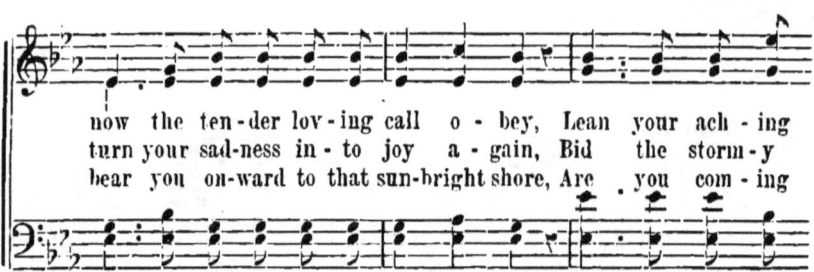

now the ten-der lov-ing call o-bey, Lean your ach-ing
turn your sad-ness in-to joy a-gain, Bid the storm-y
bear you on-ward to that sun-bright shore, Are you com-ing

CHORUS.

heart up-on his breast.
waves of life to cease. Are you com-ing? Are you com-ing?
while he calls to-day?

Copyright, 1887, by The John Church Co.

Glorious Day.

4 O sweet will be the music that in rapture we shall hear,
When eyes at last are opened, and we see the angels near,
And, oh, the bliss of meeting with the dearly loved of yore,
And then to feel that sin and death and parting are no more.

Now to Jesus Christ the Glory.

(CLOSING.)   G. F. R., by per.

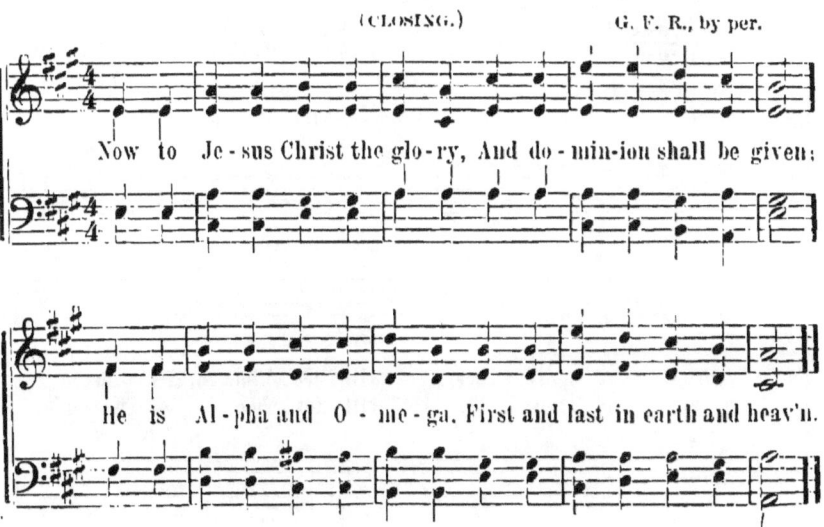

There's a Light from the Cross.

J. R. Murray.

1. There's a light from the cross, There's a light from the Word; It is flooding the earth with the joy of the Lord! And the hearts that were aching In darkness, and breaking, Are chanting his praises, in blissful accord.

2. Bow down eastern mountains, The Savior has come! And sing, O ye fountains, in ev'ry wide zone! To ev'ry dark nation The glad proclamation Is offering welcome, and pardon, and home!

3. There's a light from the cross, There's a light from the Word! And the kingdoms of earth are the realms of the Lord! O Savior victorious. So tender and glorious, We praise thee, we bless thee in reverent accord.

CHORUS.

There's a light! There's a light! from the cross, from the cross! There's a light from the cross! There's a light from the cross!

Copyright, 1887, by The John Church Co.

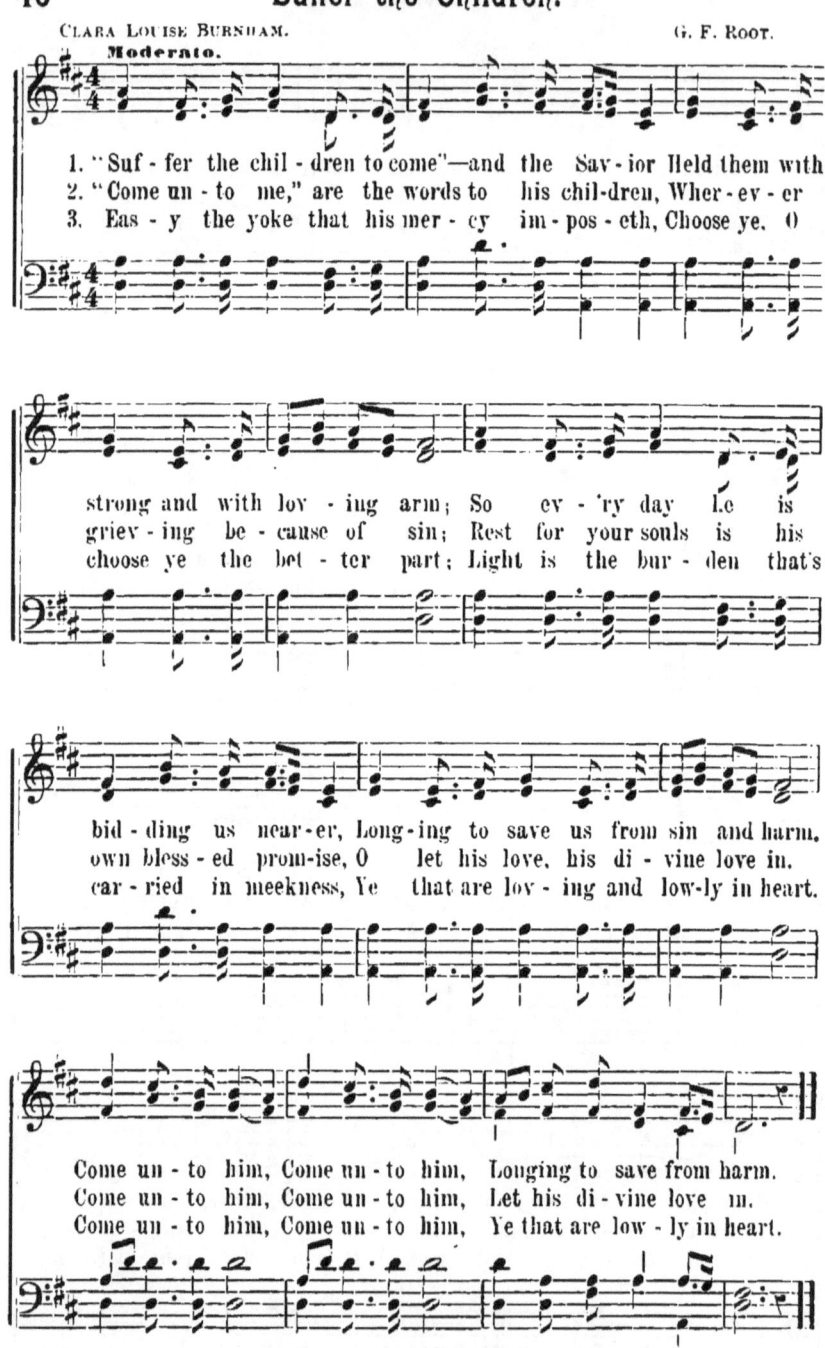

Little Gleaner's Band. 41

JULIA C. ELWELL. J. R. M

1. We're a lit-tle glean-er's band, Toil-ing day by day;
2. Bus-y boys and girls may we Toil for Af-ric wild;
3. Teach them how to praise and love, Wor-ship and o-bey.

Gath-'ring for a hea-then land Pen-nies by the way.
In-ter-est-ed we should be In each hea-then child.
Christ, the Lord, who reigns a-bove— He's the truth, the way.

Glean-ers in the mis-sion field, Like the faith-ful Ruth;
Tell them gods of wood and stone Noth-ing good can give;
We're a lit-tle glean-er's band, Toil-ing day by day;

To tempta-tion will not yield, Al-ways speak the truth.
Tell them Je-sus Christ a-lone Can their sins for-give.
Gath-'ring for a hea-then land Pen-nies by the way.

Copyright, 1888, by THE JOHN CHURCH CO.

44. Sing of Jesus.

"WINTHROP."

1. Sing of Je-sus! sing for-ev-er Of the love that changes nev-er, Who or what from him can sev-er Those he makes his own?
2. With his blood the Lord hath bought them, When they knew him not, he sought them, And from all their wand'rings brought them, His the praise alone.

REFRAIN.

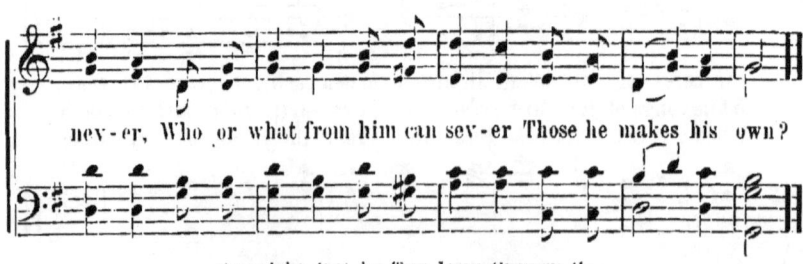

Sing of Je-sus! sing for-ev-er! Sing the love that chang-es nev-er, Who or what from him can sev-er Those he makes his own?

Copyright, 1888, by THE JOHN CHURCH CO.

In the Days of thy Youth. 47

LOWER LIGHTS.

1 Brightly beams our Father's mercy,
  From his lighthouse evermore,
  But to us he gives the keeping
  Of the lights along the shore.

CHORUS.
Let the lower lights be burning,
  Send a gleam across the wave!
Some poor struggling, fainting seaman
  You may rescue, you may save.

2 Dark the night of sin has settled;
  Loud the angry billows roar;
Eager eyes are watching, longing,
  For the lights along the shore.

3 Trim your feeble lamp, my brother;
  Some poor sailor, tempest tost,
Trying now to make the harbor,
  In the darkness may be lost.

P. P. BLISS.

JEWELS.

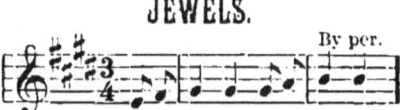

1 When he cometh, when he cometh,
  To make up his jewels,
All his jewels, precious jewels,
  His loved and his own.

CHORUS.
Like the stars of the morning,
  His bright crown adorning,
They shall shine in their beauty,
  Bright gems for his crown.

2 He will gather, he will gather,
  The gems from his kingdom;
All the pure ones, all the bright ones,
  His loved and his own.

3 Little children, little children,
  Who love their Redeemer,
Are the jewels, precious jewels,
  His loved and his own.

Rev. W. O. CUSHING.

The Master wants Workers.

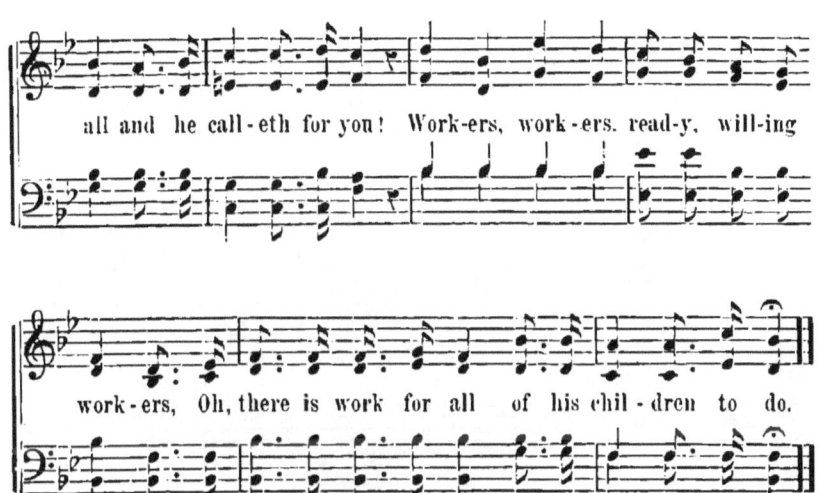

His Little Ones.

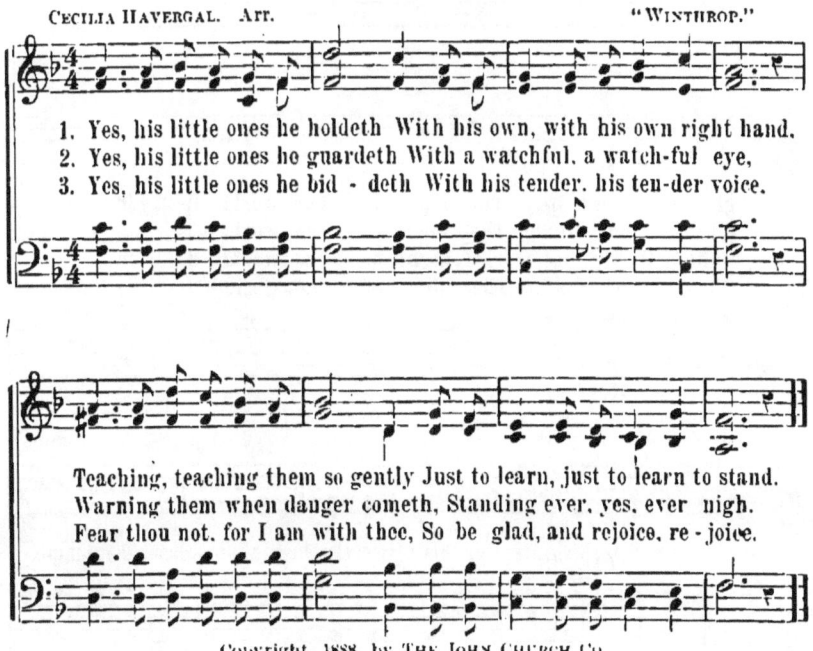

Copyright, 1888, by THE JOHN CHURCH CO.

The Light of the World is Jesus.

Once I was blind, but now I can see; The Light of the world is Je-sus.

What Hast Thou Done for Me?

"So Christ was once offered to bear the sins of many." Heb. 9: 28.

Miss FRANCES R. HAVERGAL.   P. P. BLISS, by per.

Moderato.

1. I gave my life for thee, My pre-cious blood I shed,
2. My Fa-ther's house of light— My glo-ry-cir-cled throne,

That thou might'st ransomed be, And quickened from the dead;
I left for earth-ly night, For wand'rings sad and lone;

I gave, I gave my life for thee, What hast thou given for me?
I left, I left it all for thee. Hast thou left aught for me?

3. I suffered much for thee,
More than thy tongue can tell,
Of bitterest agony,
To rescue thee from hell;
I've borne, I've borne it all for thee,
What hast thou borne for me?

4. And I have brought to thee,
Down from my home above,
Salvation full and free,
My pardon and my love;
I bring, I bring rich gifts to thee,
What hast thou brought to me?

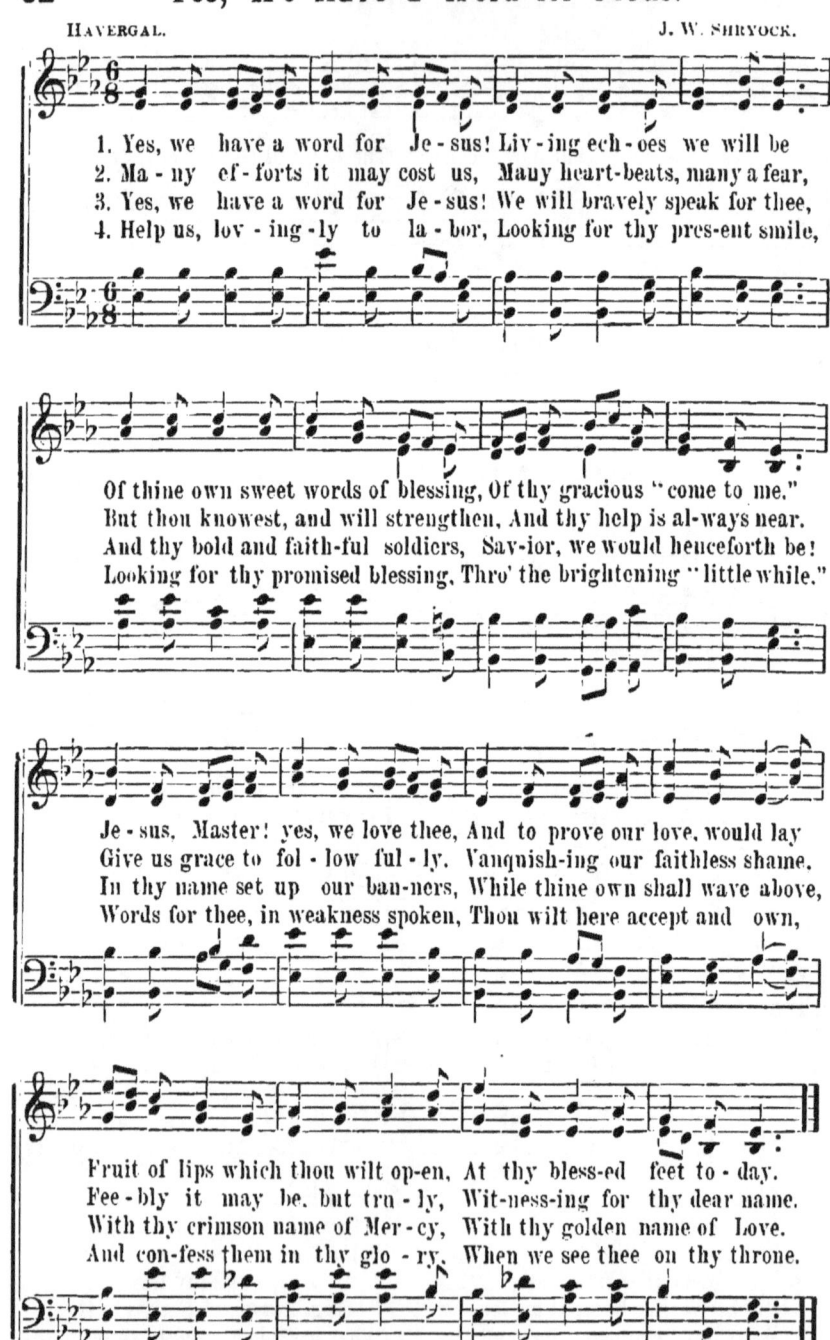

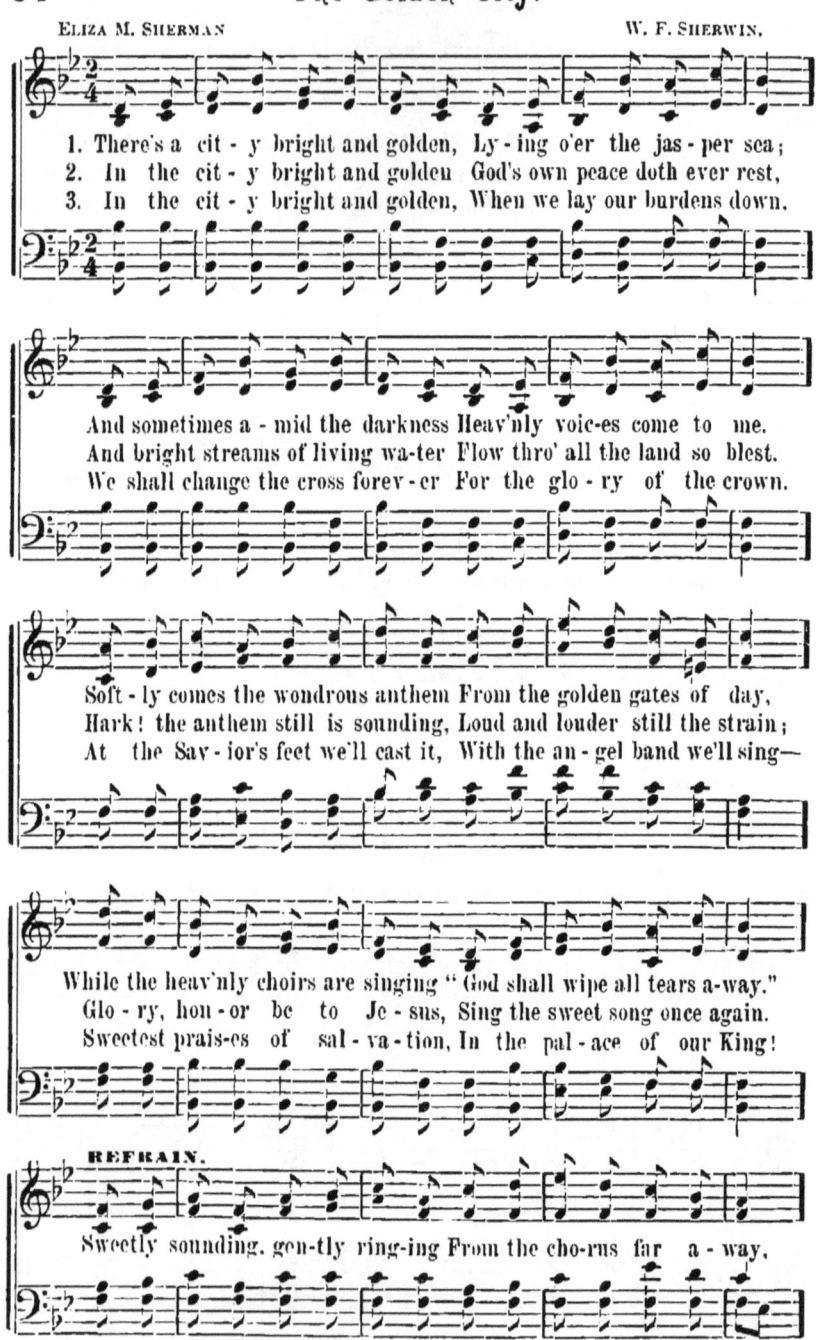

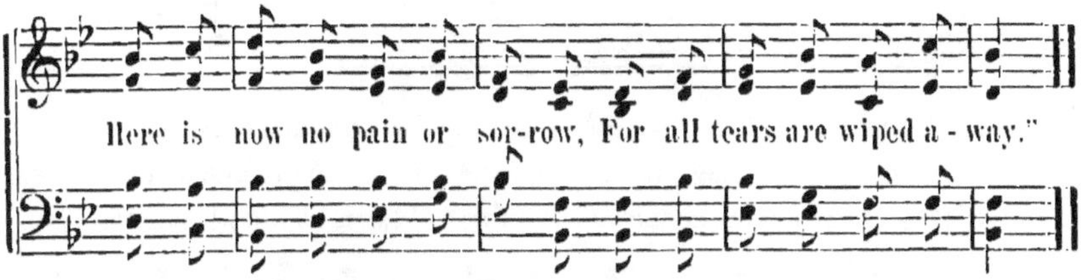

The Golden City.

Here is now no pain or sor-row, For all tears are wiped a-way."

Childhood and the Lilies.

Rev. F. M. Higginson. German.

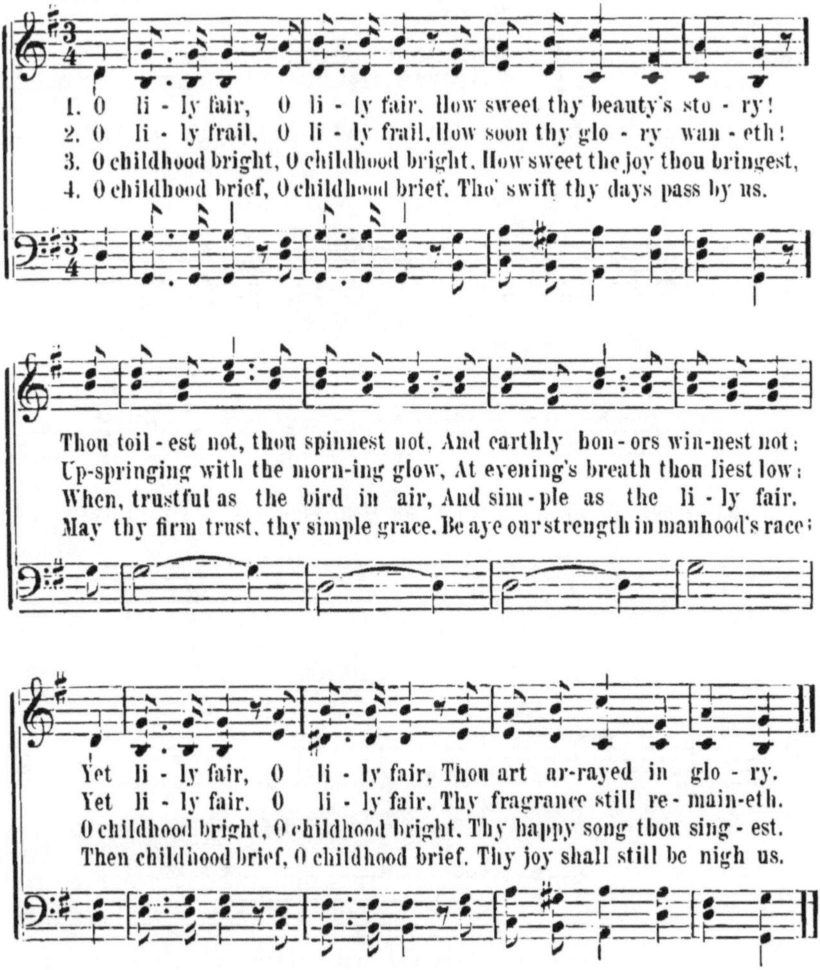

1. O li-ly fair, O li-ly fair, How sweet thy beauty's sto-ry!
2. O li-ly frail, O li-ly frail, How soon thy glo-ry wan-eth!
3. O childhood bright, O childhood bright, How sweet the joy thou bringest,
4. O childhood brief, O childhood brief, Tho' swift thy days pass by us.

Thou toil-est not, thou spinnest not, And earthly hon-ors win-nest not;
Up-springing with the morn-ing glow, At evening's breath thou liest low;
When, trustful as the bird in air, And sim-ple as the li-ly fair,
May thy firm trust, thy simple grace, Be aye our strength in manhood's race;

Yet li-ly fair, O li-ly fair, Thou art ar-rayed in glo-ry.
Yet li-ly fair, O li-ly fair, Thy fragrance still re-main-eth.
O childhood bright, O childhood bright, Thy happy song thou sing-est.
Then childhood brief, O childhood brief, Thy joy shall still be nigh us.

56. Thy Word, O Lord, a Lantern is.

ALICE M. SCHOFF.   J. R. M.

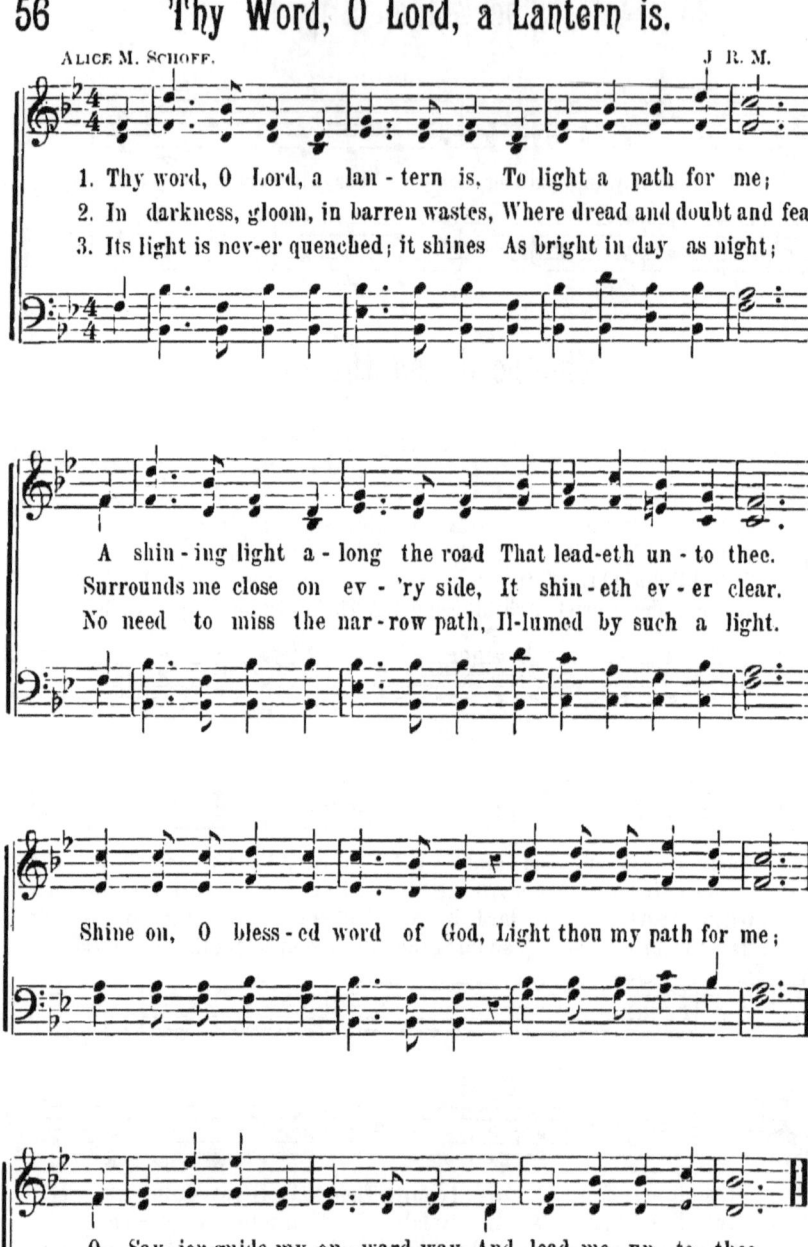

1. Thy word, O Lord, a lan-tern is, To light a path for me;
2. In darkness, gloom, in barren wastes, Where dread and doubt and fear
3. Its light is nev-er quenched; it shines As bright in day as night;

A shin-ing light a-long the road That lead-eth un-to thee.
Surrounds me close on ev-'ry side, It shin-eth ev-er clear.
No need to miss the nar-row path, Il-lumed by such a light.

Shine on, O bless-ed word of God, Light thou my path for me;
O Sav-ior guide my on-ward way, And lead me up to thee.

Copyright, 1888, by THE JOHN CHURCH CO.

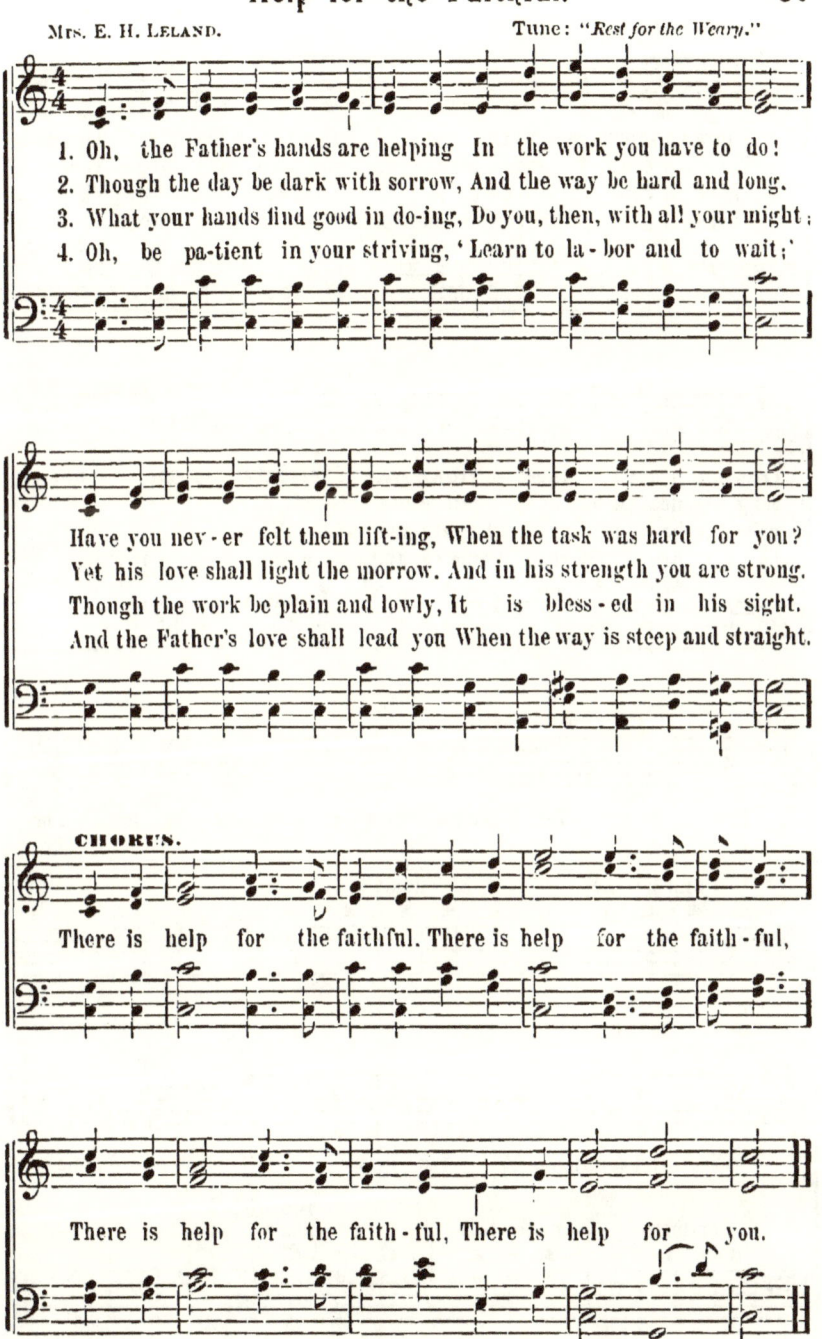

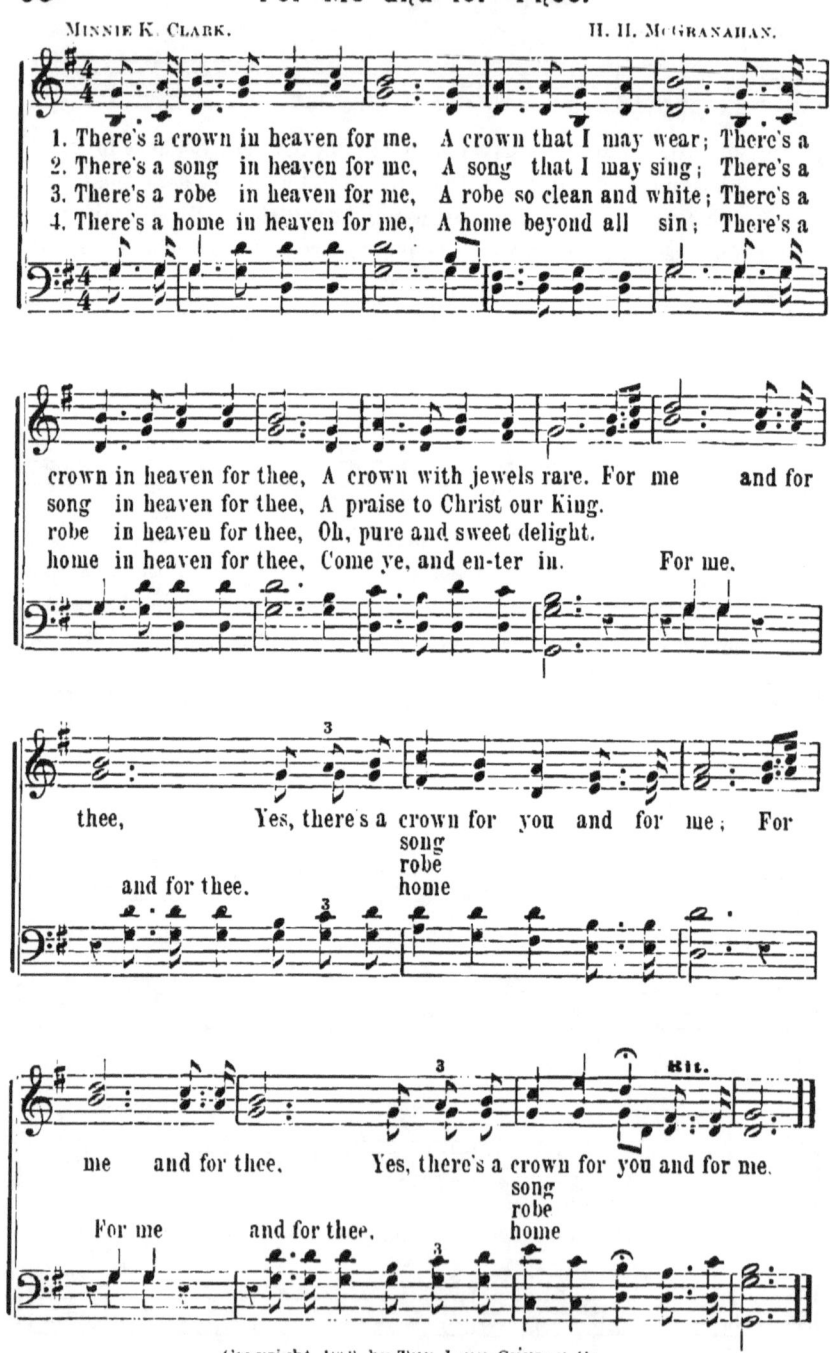

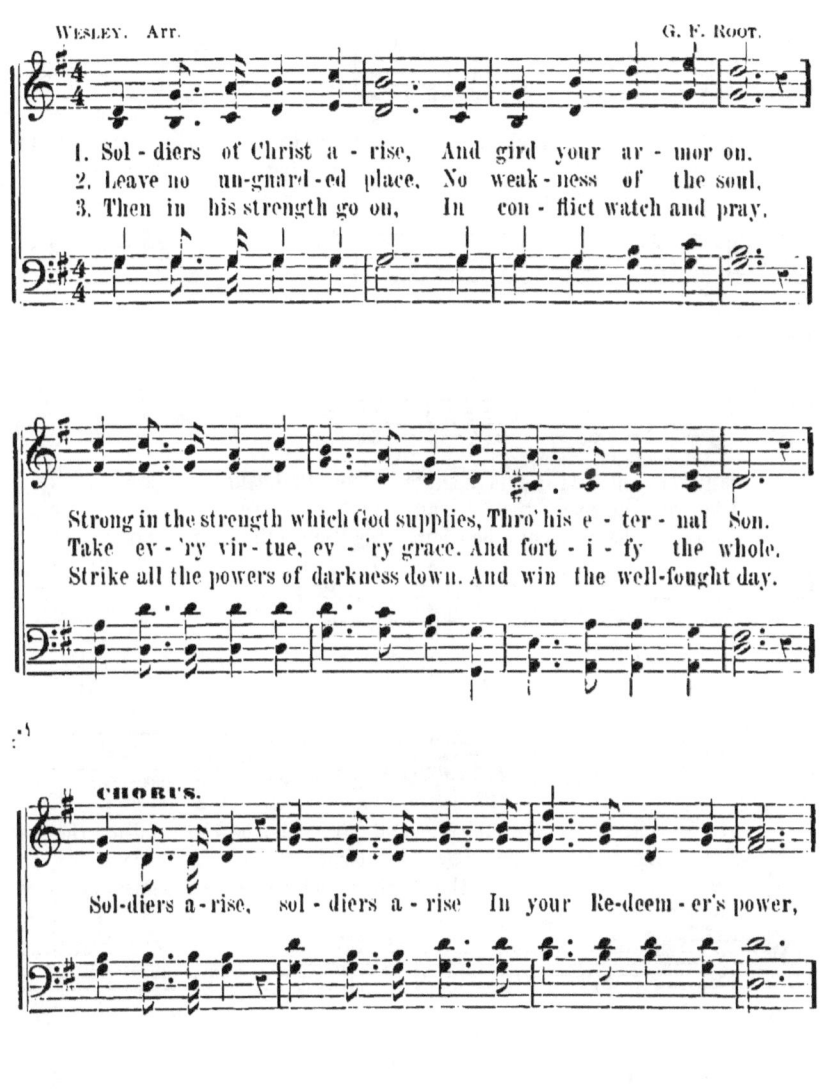

Waiting for Me.

Holiness Becometh Thine House.

SENTENCE. H. H. QUICK.

Copyright, 1888, by THE JOHN CHURCH CO.

Beautiful Land on High.

In that beautiful land I'll be, I'll be From earth and its cares set free, set free;
My Jesus is there, He's gone to prepare A place in that land for me, for me.

Praise Ye the Father.

Mrs. Elisabeth Charles.　　　Frederick Ferdinand Flemming.

1. Praise ye the Fa-ther for his lov-ing kindness, Ten-der-ly cares he for his lov-ing chil-dren; Praise him, ye an-gels, praise him in the heav-ens, Praise ye Je-ho-vah!
2. Praise ye the Sav-ior, great is his com-pas-sion, Gracious-ly cares he for his chos-en peo-ple; Young men and maid-ens, ye old men and chil-dren, Praise ye the Sav-ior!
3. Praise ye the Spir-it, Com-fort-er of Is-rael, Sent of the Fa-ther and the Son to bless us; Praise ye the Fa-ther, Son, and Ho-ly Spir-it, Praise ye the Tri-une God!

68. O Beulah, Land of Beulah!

"They shall behold the land that is very far off." Isa. 33: 17.

H. L. Frisbie.
G. F. R.

Moderato.

1. We stand where Jordan's waves divide—O Beu-lah, land of Beu-lah—
2. We look a-cross the rag-ing foam—O Beu-lah, land of Beu-lah—
3. No mor-tal foot hath ev-er trod— O Beu-lah, land of Beu-lah—

The shores of time from Canaan's side, Sweet Beulah, land of Beu-lah;
With ea-ger longings for our home In Beu-lah, land of Beu-lah;
The glorious dwelling-place of God, In Beu-lah, land of Beu-lah;

On that fair shore no shade of night, The hills are crowned with fadeless light;
No ear hath heard, no eye hath seen, The wondrous songs, the joy serene,
Im-mor-tal on-ly those who sing The praises of our glorious King,

Blind faith will lose her-self in sight—Sweet Beulah, land of Beu-lah.
The land of hills and valleys green, Sweet Beulah, land of Beu-lah.
In an-thems that shall ev-er ring In Beu-lah, land of Beu-lah.

Copyright, 1888, by The John Church Co.

O Beulah, Land of Beulah!

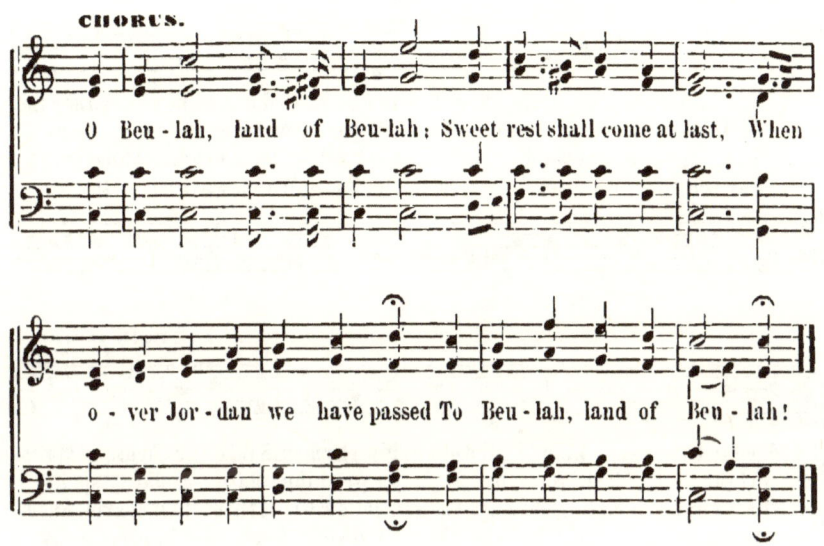

God is Love.

"He that loveth not knoweth not God, for God is love." 1 John 4: 8.

G. F. ROOT.

Copyright, 1888, by the JOHN CHURCH Co.

70. Kind Words Can Never Die.

From "The Athenæum."  Sister Abby? (Hutchinson Family.)

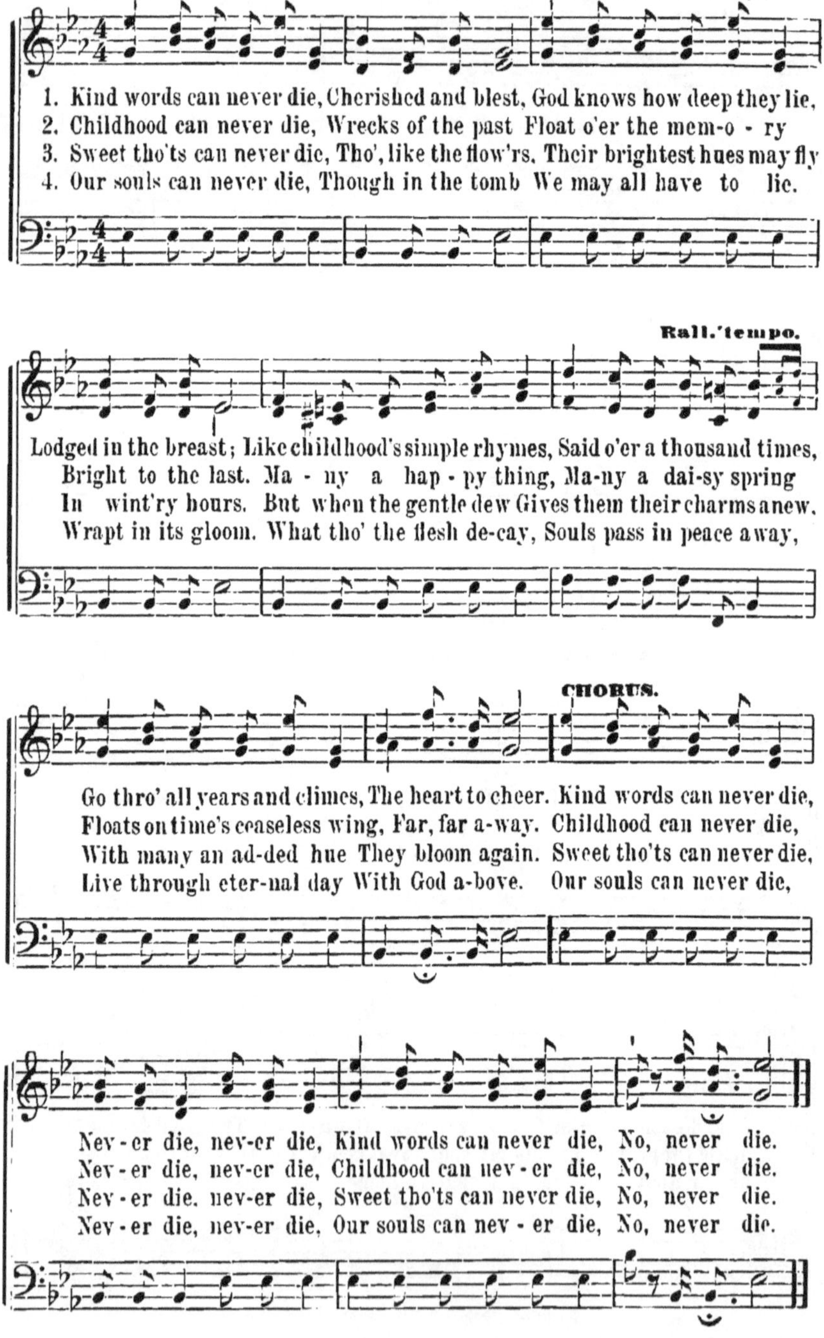

1. Kind words can never die, Cherished and blest, God knows how deep they lie, Lodged in the breast; Like childhood's simple rhymes, Said o'er a thousand times, Go thro' all years and climes, The heart to cheer. Kind words can never die, Nev-er die, nev-er die, Kind words can never die, No, never die.

2. Childhood can never die, Wrecks of the past Float o'er the mem-o-ry Bright to the last. Ma-ny a hap-py thing, Ma-ny a dai-sy spring Floats on time's ceaseless wing, Far, far a-way. Childhood can never die, Nev-er die, nev-er die, Childhood can nev-er die, No, never die.

3. Sweet tho'ts can never die, Tho', like the flow'rs, Their brightest hues may fly In wint'ry hours. But when the gentle dew Gives them their charms anew, With many an ad-ded hue They bloom again. Sweet tho'ts can never die, Nev-er die, nev-er die, Sweet tho'ts can never die, No, never die.

4. Our souls can never die, Though in the tomb We may all have to lie, Wrapt in its gloom. What tho' the flesh de-cay, Souls pass in peace away, Live through eter-nal day With God a-bove. Our souls can never die, Nev-er die, nev-er die, Our souls can nev-er die, No, never die.

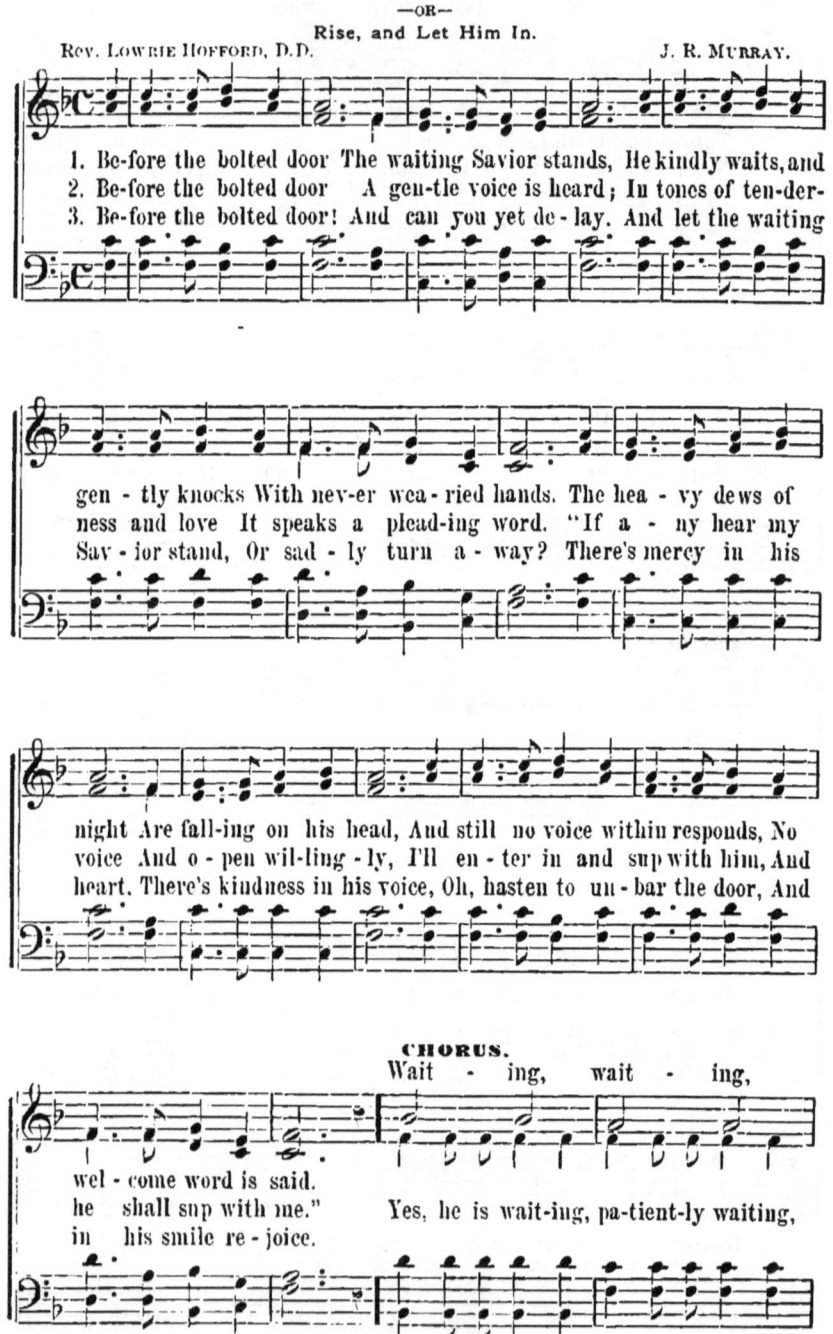

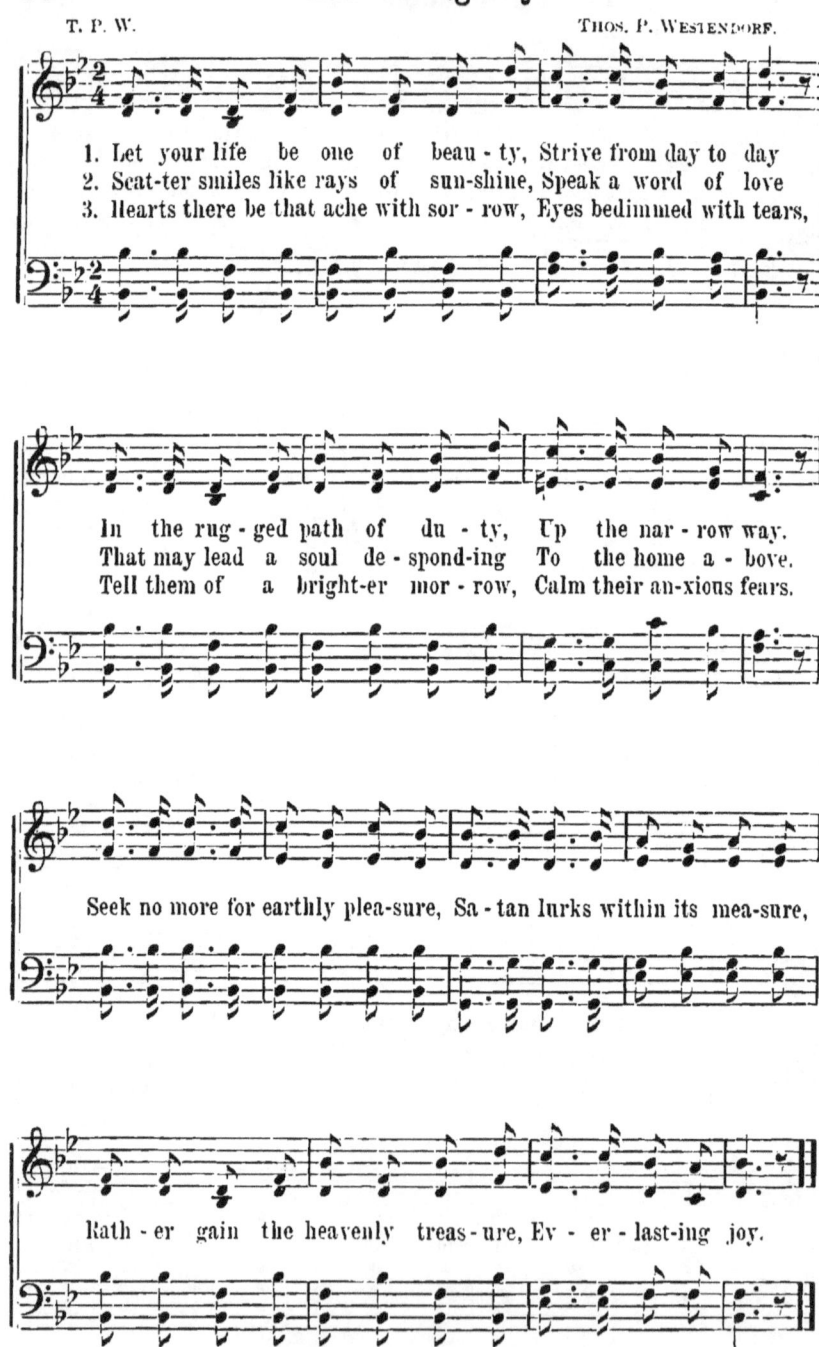

The Thought of Jesus.   77

BERNARD. G. F. ROOT.

1. No voice can sing, no mind can frame, Nor can the mem-'ry find
A sweet-er sound than Je-sus' name, The Sav-ior of man-kind.

2. O hope of ev-'ry contrite heart, O joy of all the meek,
To those who fall how kind thou art, How good to those who seek!

3. But what to those who find? ah! this Nor tongue, nor pen can show;
The love of Je-sus what it is, None but his loved ones know.

CHORUS.

Je-sus, the ve-ry thought of thee With sweetness fills the breast,
But sweet-er far thy face to see, And in thy presence rest.

Copyright, 1888, by THE JOHN CHURCH CO.

78. The Hope of Glory.

H. R. Y.
Helen R. Young.

1. What to me are all life's pleasures? What is all its wealth and pride?
2. O my Sav-ior, thee possess-ing, All the wealth of heav'n is mine;
3. Child of God and heir of heav-en, O the won-ders of his love!

Give to me the hid-den treas-ures, Let me in my Lord a-bide.
Je-sus Christ my name confess-ing, O my soul, canst thou re-pine?
O how great the mer-cy giv-en, Coming down from heav'n above.

REFRAIN.

Christ in me, the hope of glo-ry, Hid-den mys-te-ry di-vine,

Let me tell the wondrous sto-ry, I am his and he is mine.

Copyright, 1888, by The John Church Co.

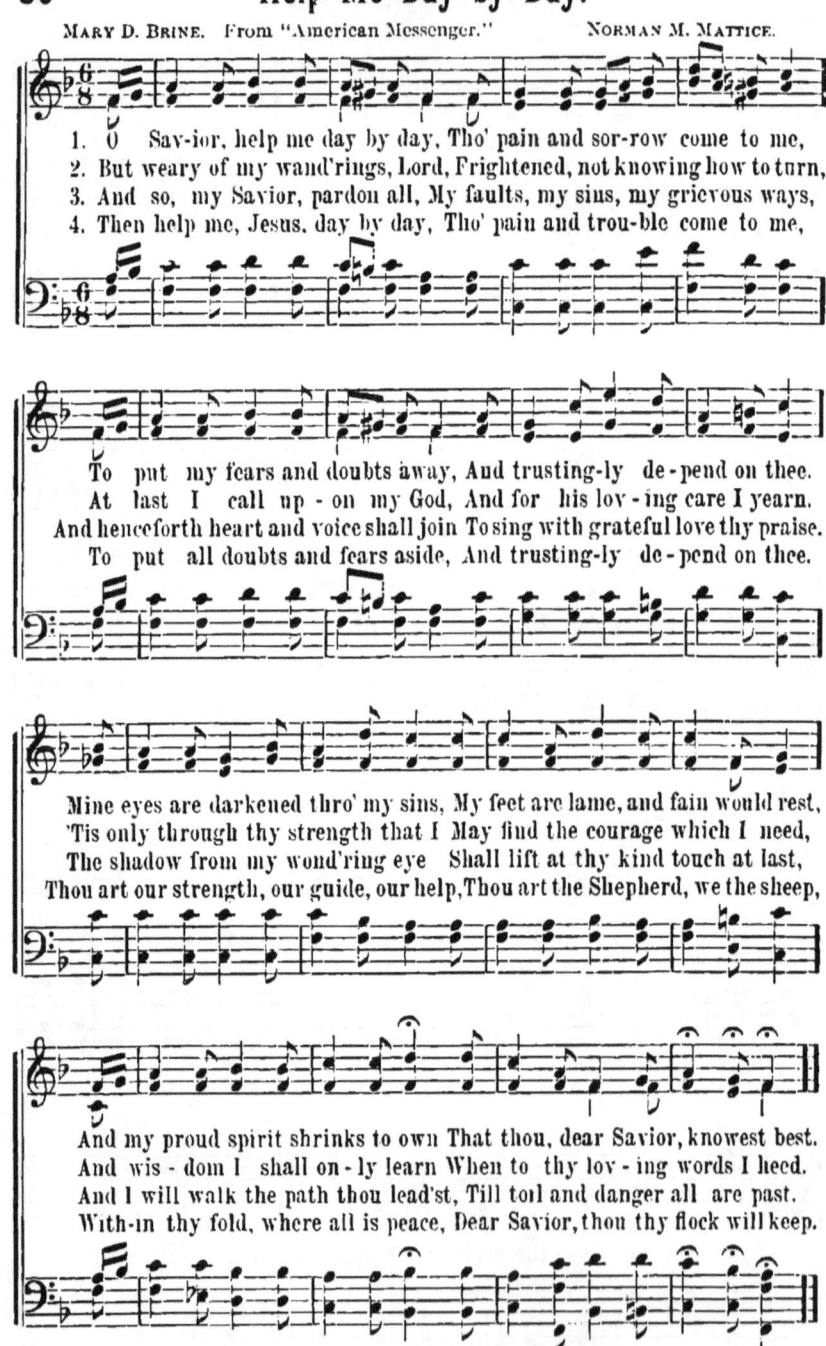

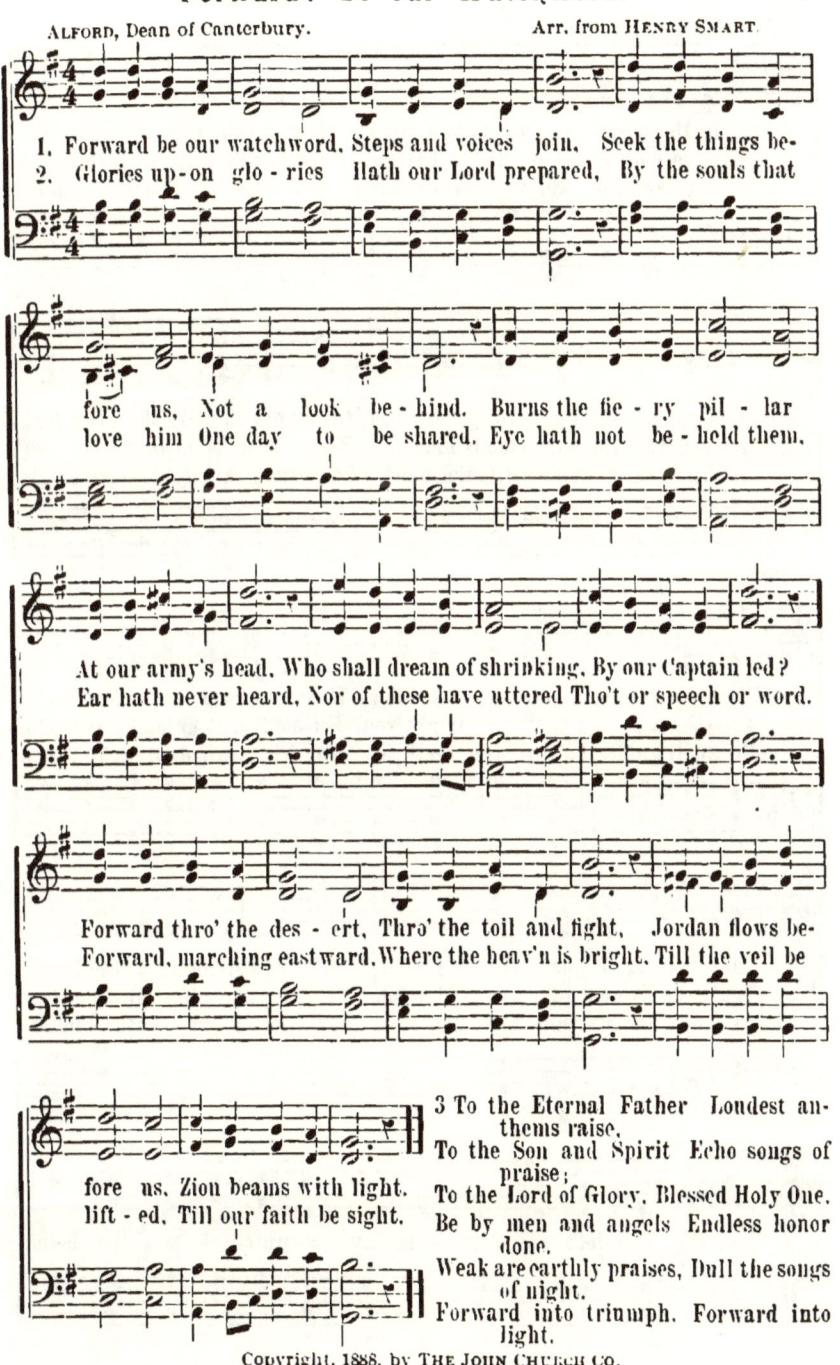

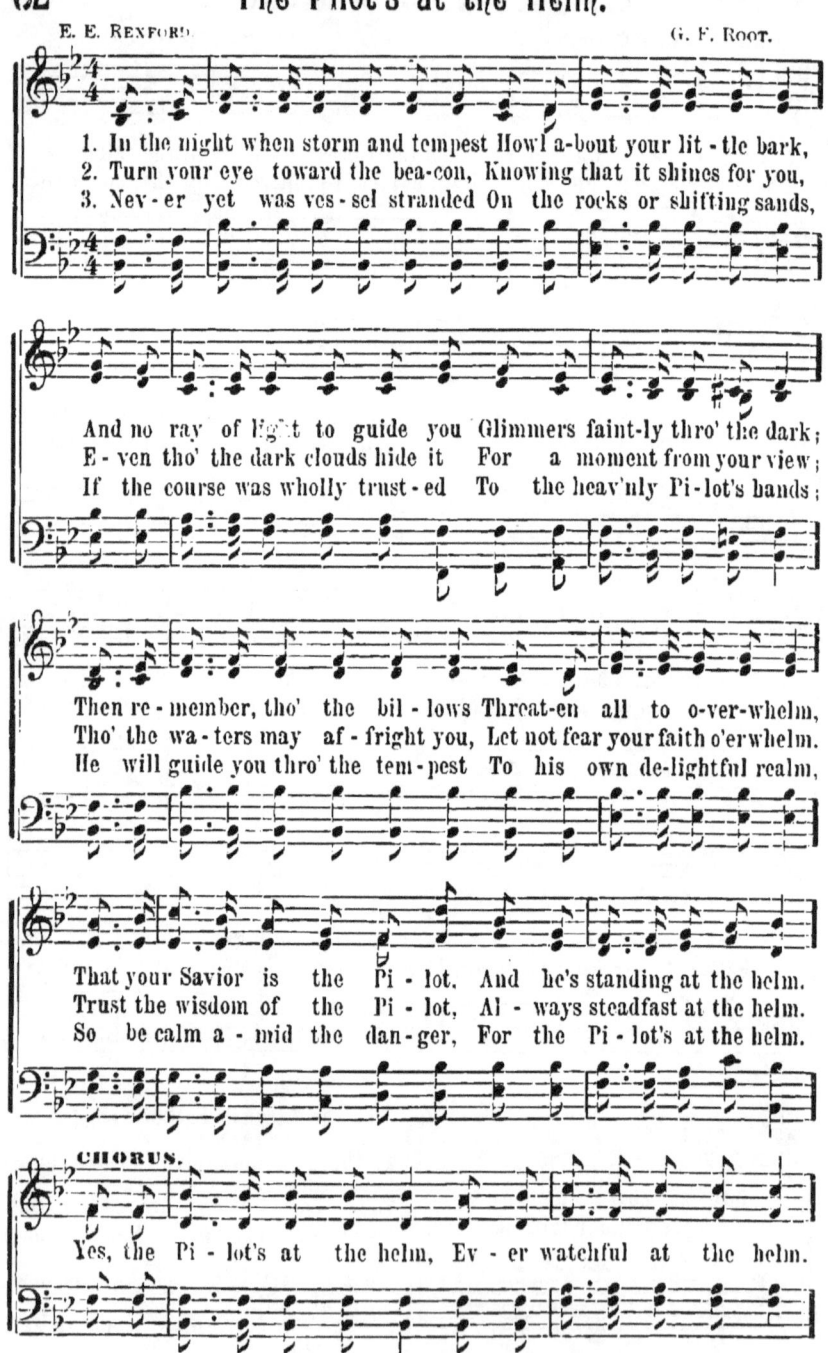

The Pilot's at the Helm.

And no storms can o-ver-whelm you While he's standing at the helm.

Forward, March.

THEO. MONOD. W. F. SHERWIN.

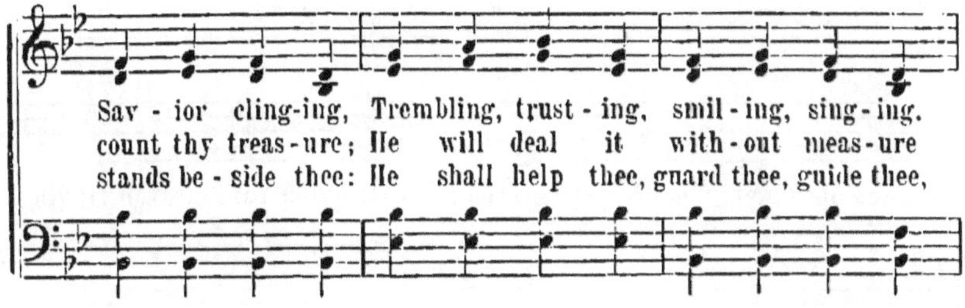

1. For-ward, march! For-ward, march! Sin - ner, to the
Sav - ior cling-ing, Trembling, trust-ing, smil-ing, sing-ing.
Hark! a - gain his voice is ring-ing, "For - ward march!"

2. For-ward, march! For-ward, march! Tar - ry not to
count thy treas-ure; He will deal it with-out meas-ure
As thou do - est his good pleas-ure— For - ward march!

3. For-ward, march! For-ward, march! Art thou faint? he
stands be - side thee: He shall help thee, guard thee, guide thee,
In his sha - dow he shall hide thee— For - ward march!

4 Forward march! Forward march!
Through th' allurements of temptation,
Through the fires of tribulation,
Holding forth the great salvation,
  Forward march!

5 Forward march! Forward march!
Till thy bending head be hoary,
Till shall close thine earthly story,
Till thou step from grace to glory,
  Forward march!

Copyright, 1888, by THE JOHN CHURCH CO.

84. When Jesus Comes.

"Unto them that look for him shall he appear the second time, without sin, unto salvation." Heb. 9: 28.

P. P. B.   P. P. BLISS, by per.

1. Down life's dark vale we wander, Till Jesus comes; We watch and wait and wonder, Till Jesus comes.
2. Oh, let my lamp be burning, When Jesus comes; For him my soul be yearning, When Jesus comes.
3. No more heart-pangs nor sadness, When Jesus comes; All peace and joy and gladness, When Jesus comes.
4. All doubts and fears will vanish, When Jesus comes; All gloom his face will banish, When Jesus comes.

CHORUS.

All joy his loved ones bringing, When Jesus comes; All praise thro' heaven ringing, When Jesus comes. All beauty bright and vernal, When Jesus comes; All glory, grand. eternal, When Jesus comes.

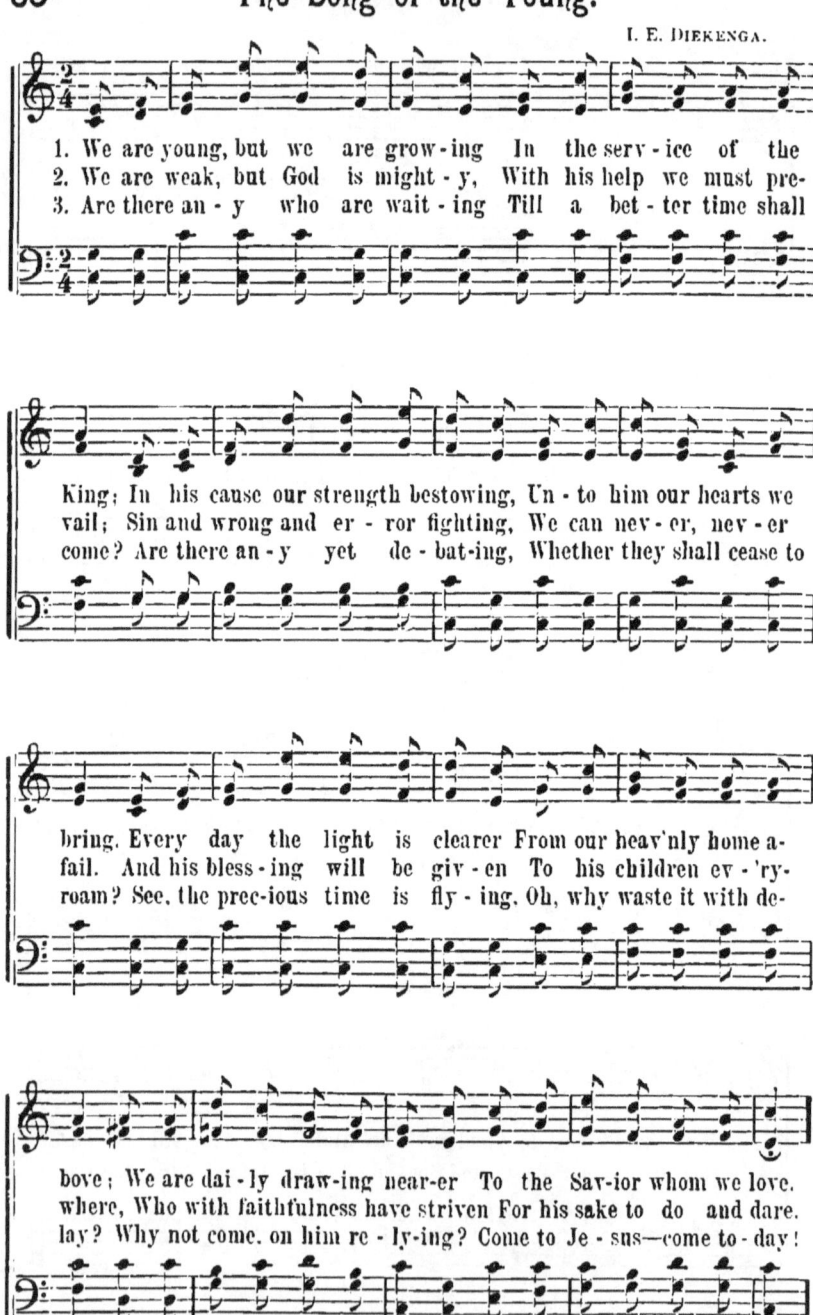

The Song of the Young.

Dismission.
(SICILY.)

Lord, dismiss us with thy blessing,
  Fill our hearts with joy and peace;
Let us each, thy love possessing,
  Triumph in redeeming grace.
    O refresh us,
Traveling through this wilderness.

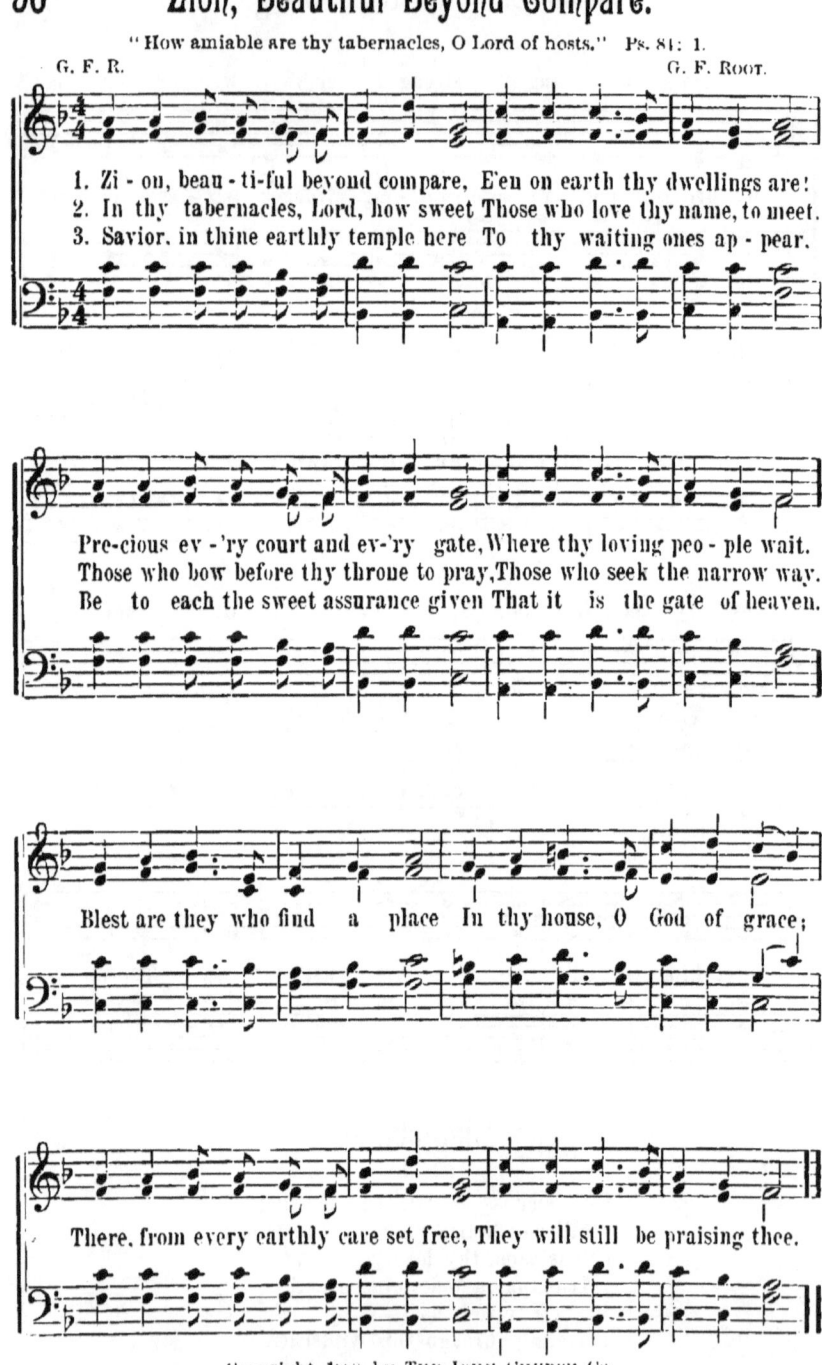

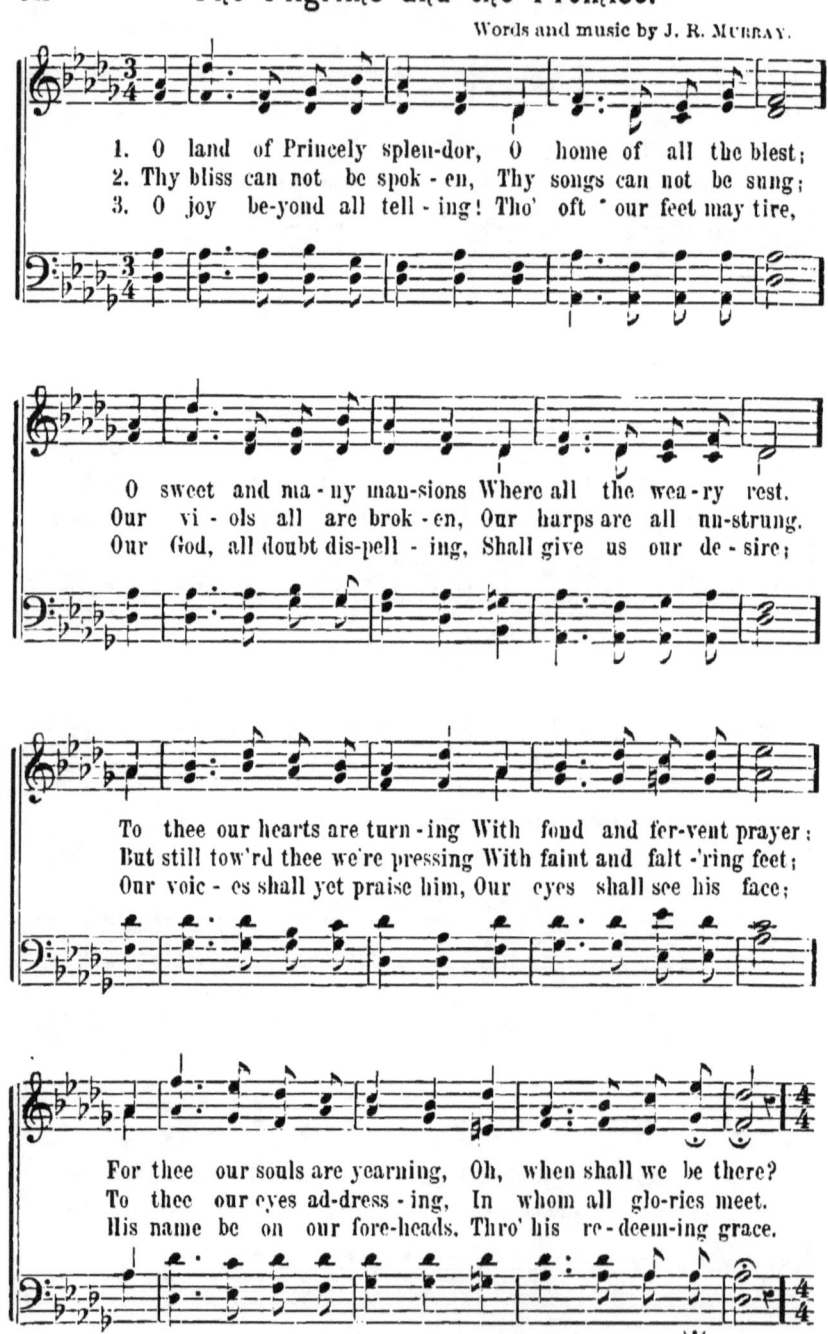

The Pilgrims and the Promise.

REFRAIN. (*May be sung by an invisible chorus.*)

Wait, wait, Wait, O wait, yes, wait up-on the Lord, He shall give thee thy hearts' de-sire; Wait, O wait, yes, O wait, yes, wait, wait, wait up-on the Lord, He shall give thee thy hearts' de-sire, O wait.

The Lord is Gracious.

Chant.

1. The Lord is gra-cious, and full of compassion; Slow to anger, and of great mercy.
2. The Lord is good to all, And his mer-cies are o-ver all his works.
3. All thy works shall praise thee, O Lord, And thy saints shall bless thee.

96. Hallelujah! Praise the Lord.

G. H. S.   Geo. H. Simmons.

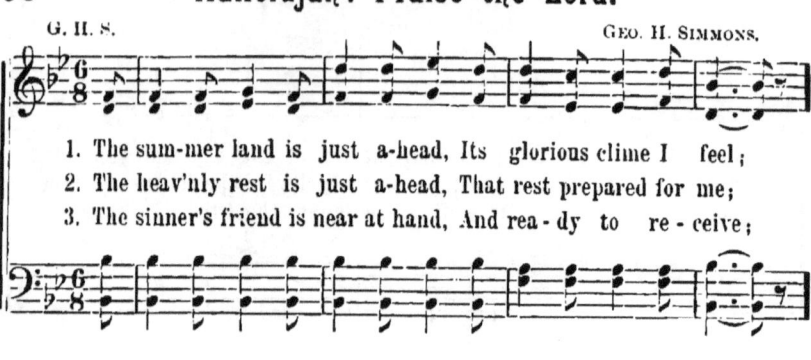

1. The sum-mer land is just a-head, Its glorious clime I feel;
2. The heav'nly rest is just a-head, That rest prepared for me;
3. The sinner's friend is near at hand, And rea-dy to re-ceive;

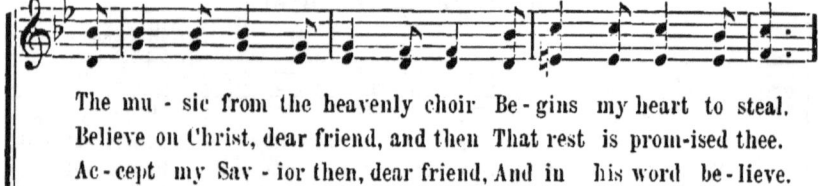

The mu - sic from the heavenly choir Be - gins my heart to steal.
Believe on Christ, dear friend, and then That rest is prom-ised thee.
Ac - cept my Sav - ior then, dear friend, And in his word be - lieve.

CHORUS.

Oh, hal - le - lu - jah! praise the Lord, Tempta - tion soon must flee;

And then by faith I'll soar a - loft To be, dear Lord, with thee.

Copyright, 1888, by The John Church Co.

Wonderful Words of Life.

"The words that I speak unto you, they are spirit, and they are life." John 6: 61.

P. P. B. P. P. Bliss, by per.

1. Sing them o-ver a-gain to me, Won-der-ful words of
2. Christ, the blessed One, gives to all Won-der-ful words of
3. Sweet-ly ech-o the gos-pel call, Won-der-ful words of

Life, Let me more of their beau-ty see, Wonder-ful words of
Life; Sin-ner, list to the lov-ing call, Wonder-ful words of
Life, Of-fer par-don and peace to all, Wonder-ful words of

Life. Words of life and beau-ty, Teach me faith and du-ty;
Life. All so free-ly giv - en, Woo-ing us to heav-en,
Life. Je - sus, on - ly Sav - ior, Sanc - ti - fy for - ev - er,

Beautiful words, wonderful words, Wonderful words of Life. Life.

Times of Refreshing.

The Sinners' Friend.

E. A. C.
Rev. Edward A. Collier.

1. Je - sus, thou art the sin - ners' friend, Lov - ing us ten - der - ly till the end; Bear - ing most pa - tient - ly with our sin, Seek - ing by love our love to win.
2. Je - sus, thou art the Lamb of God, Pass - ing re - sign - ed - ly 'neath the rod; Spot - less and meek to the al - tar led, Sac - ri - ficed there in sin - ners' stead.

3 Jesus, our Shepherd good, thou art,
Bearing the feeble ones on thy heart;
Seeking the erring with care untold,
Leading them home to thy sure fold.

4 Jesus, thou art the Prince of Peace,
Hearing thy bidding, life's tumults cease;
Speak thou to us as to wind and sea,
Great in our hearts the calm shall be.

5 Jesus, thou art the King of kings,
Hasten thy glory on time's swift wings;
Gather all diadems on thy brow,
King of our hearts, to thee we bow,

Copyright, 1888, by The John Church Co.

100 Jesus Christ, our Savior.

W. WHITING. J. B. CALKIN.

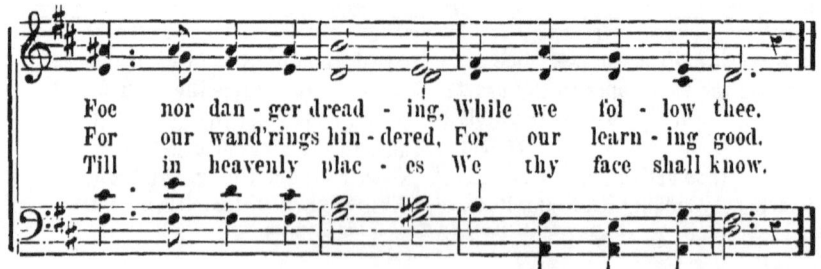

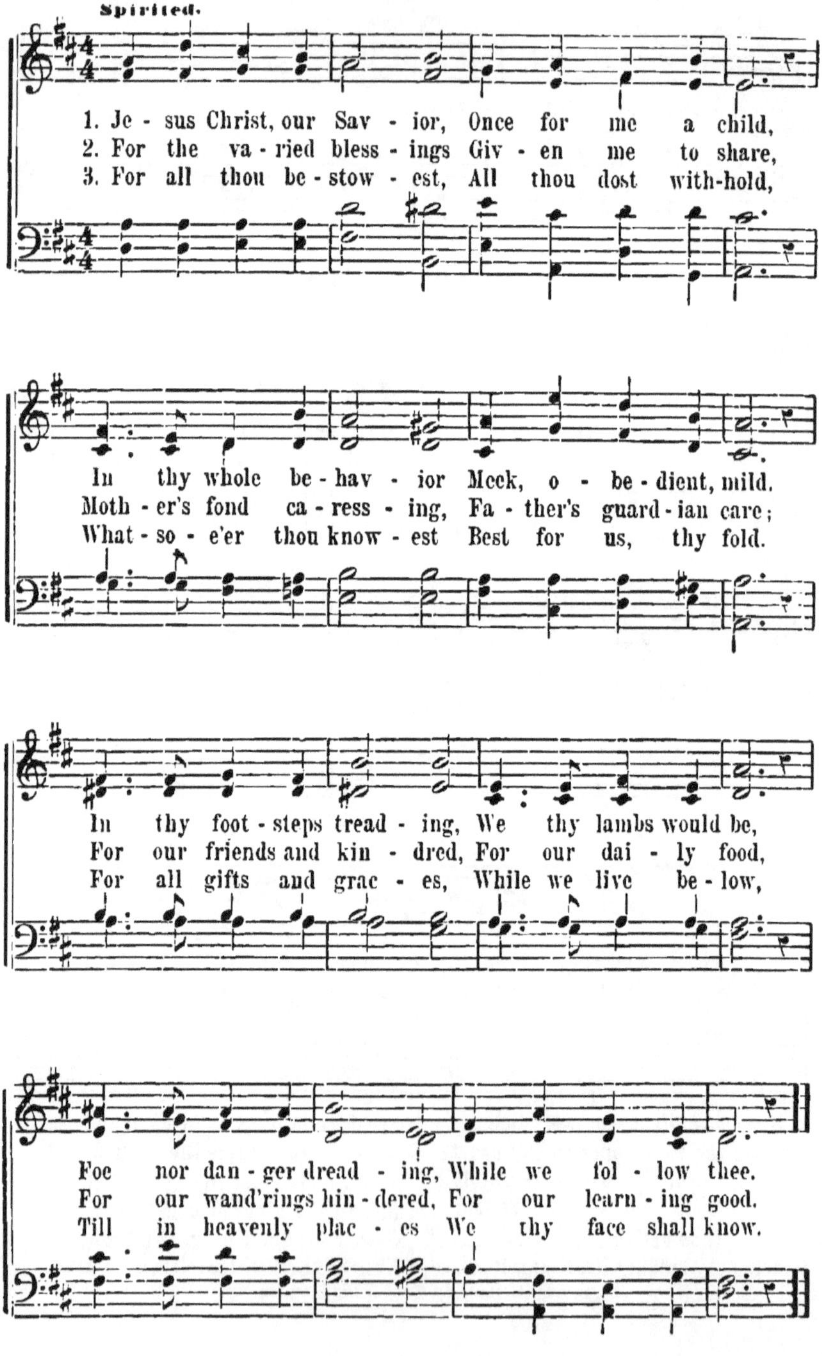

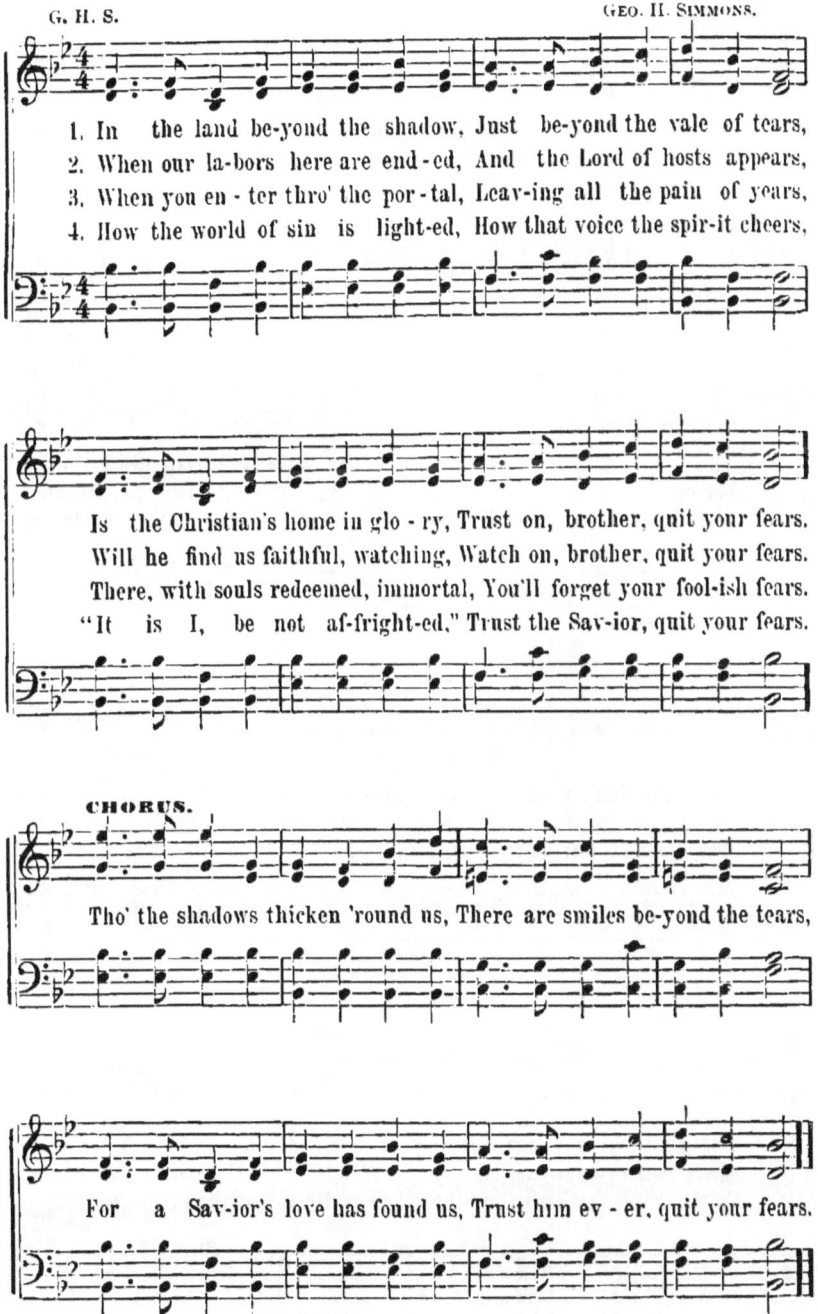

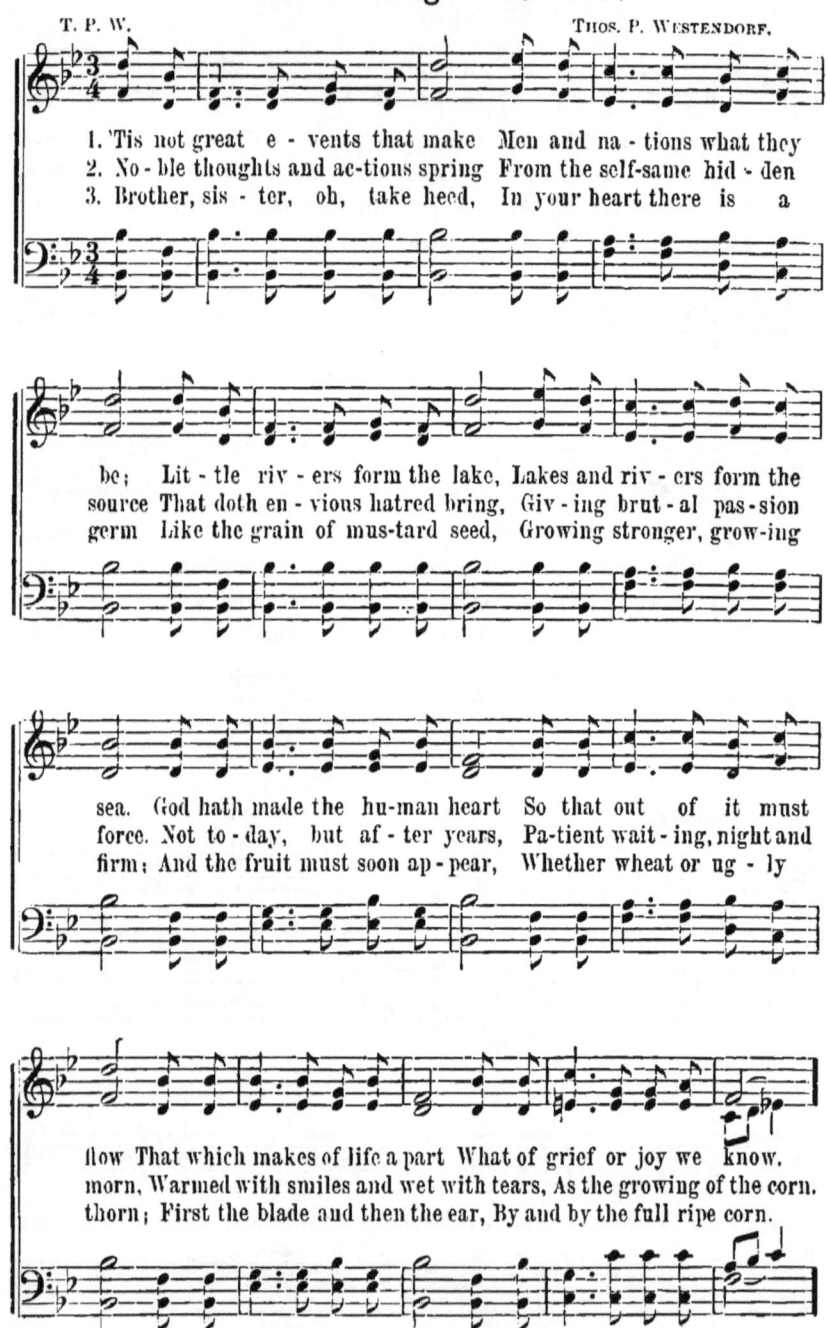

As the Growing of the Corn.

The Lord's Prayer.

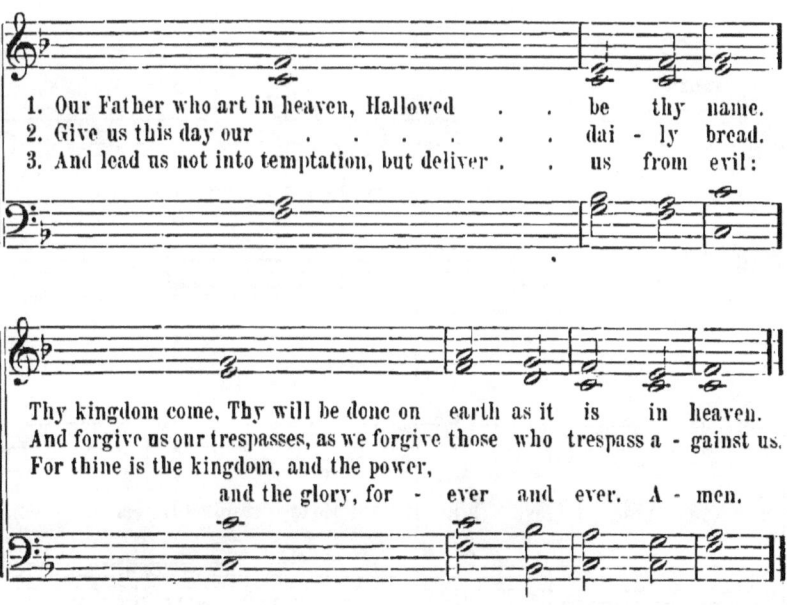

Are You One of the Ninety and Nine? 107

way, Are you sure there's no dan-ger of fall-ing, If
sin? Oh, list to the good shep-herd call-ing. He's
old; Then let not the wick-ed en-slave you. Oh,

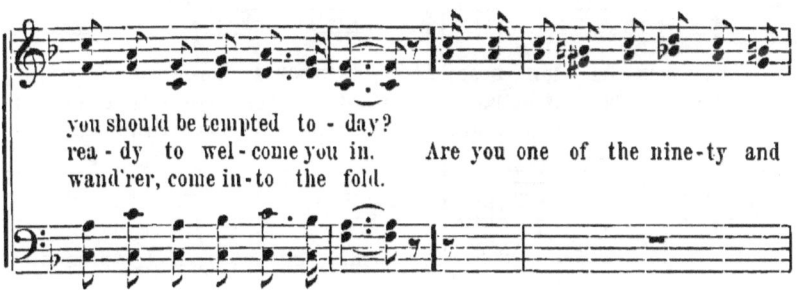

you should be tempted to-day?
rea-dy to wel-come you in. Are you one of the nine-ty and
wand'rer, come in-to the fold.

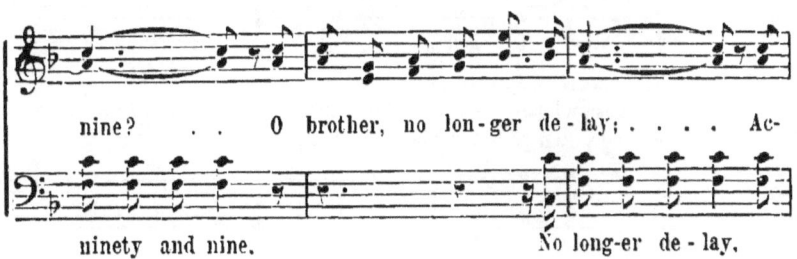

nine? .. O brother, no lon-ger de-lay; .... Ac-
ninety and nine. No long-er de-lay,

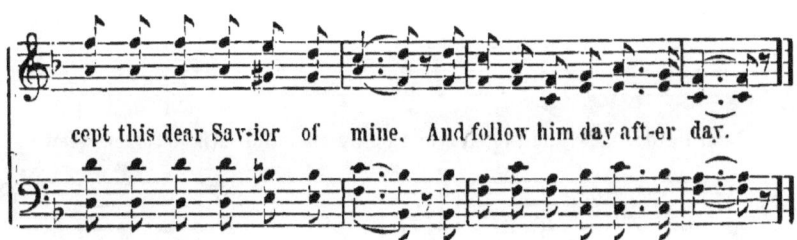

cept this dear Sav-ior of mine. And follow him day aft-er day.

108. Endeavor.

Words and music by Rev. C. H. Oliphant.

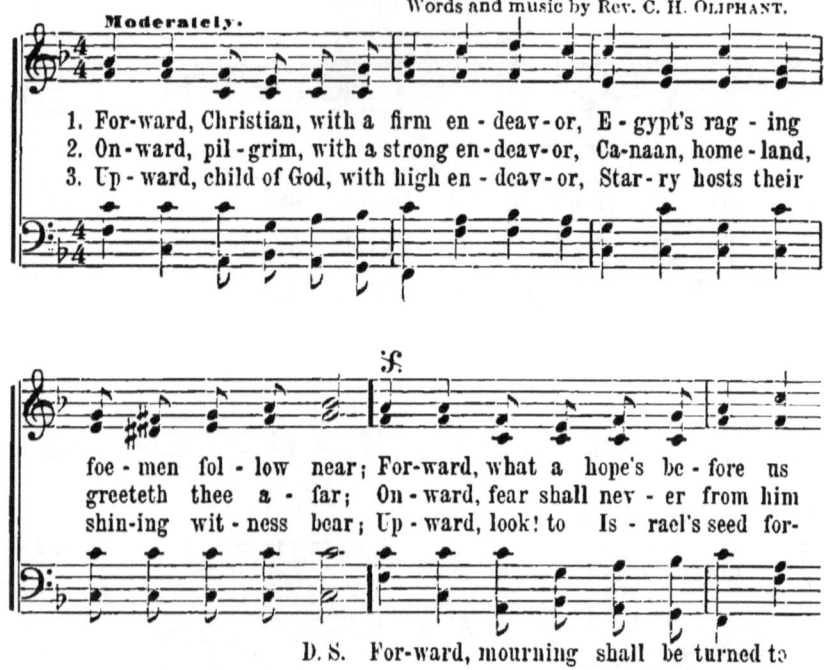

1. For-ward, Christian, with a firm en-deav-or, E-gypt's rag-ing foe-men fol-low near; For-ward, what a hope's be-fore us ev-er, What a Cap-tain have we here!
2. On-ward, pil-grim, with a strong en-deav-or, Ca-naan, home-land, greeteth thee a-far; On-ward, fear shall nev-er from him sev-er, Those who Je-sus' sol-diers are.
3. Up-ward, child of God, with high en-deav-or, Star-ry hosts their shin-ing wit-ness bear; Up-ward, look! to Is-rael's seed for-ev-er, God's own presence they de-clare.

D. S. For-ward, mourning shall be turned to

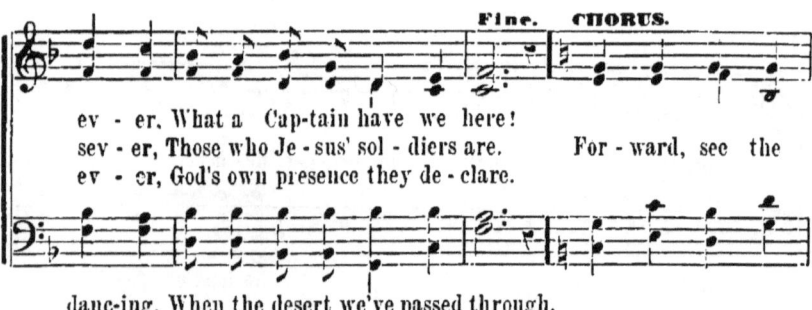

CHORUS.

For-ward, see the cloud by day ad-vanc-ing, Night the sig-nal hid-eth not from view:

danc-ing, When the desert we've passed through.

Copyright, 1887, by C. H. Oliphant.

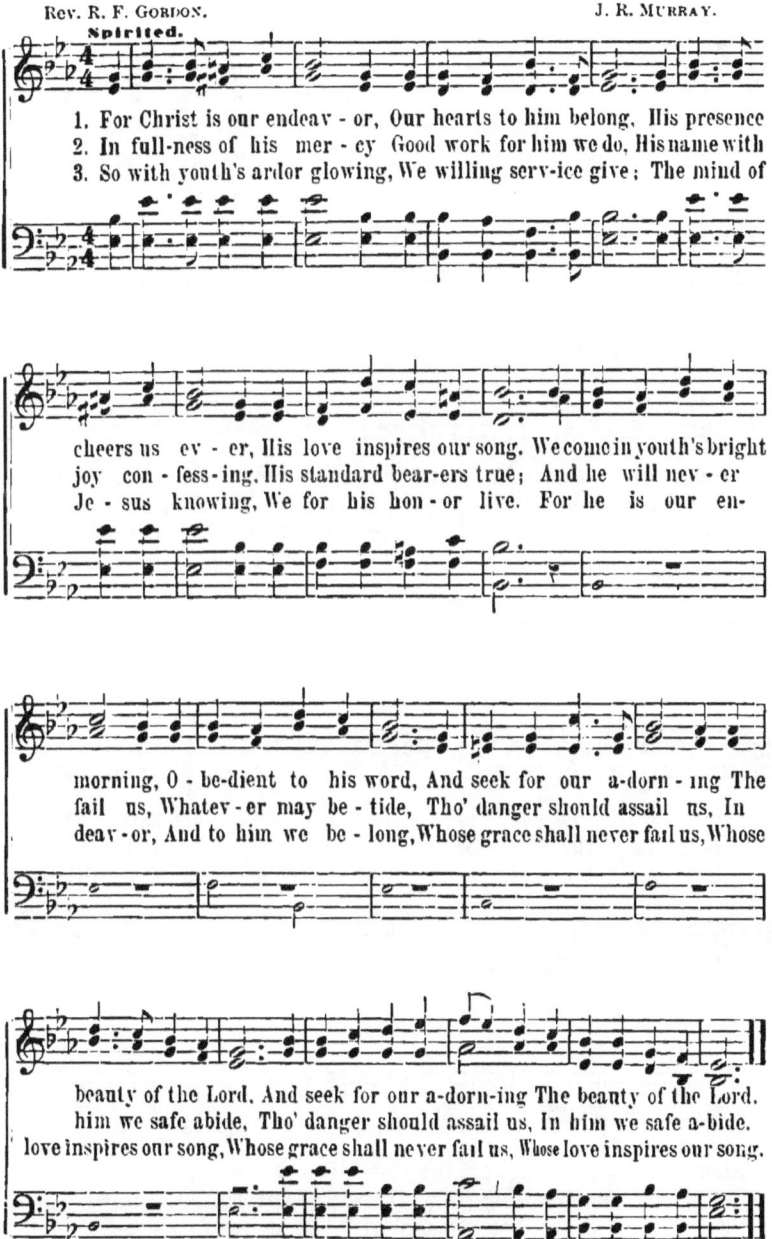

Who is the Hero?

111

lieves in God's wis-dom and might, And like sol-dier de-fend-eth the Truth and the Right, And like Sol-dier de-fend-eth the Truth and the Right.

Once He Came.

M. WEISS.   "WINTHROP."

1. Once he came in bless-ing, All our ills re-dress-ing—
Came in like-ness low-ly, Son of God most ho-ly;
Bore the cross to save us; Hope and free-dom gave us.

2. Still he comes with-in us; Still his voice would win us
From the sins that hurt us, Would to Truth con-vert us
From our fool-ish er-rors. Ere he comes in ter-rors.

Copyright, 1888, by THE JOHN CHURCH Co.

Fall Into Line. 115

fare with Sa-tan to-day; Arm for the con-flict and march to the fray.

He Remembers Me.

ERNEST W. SHURTLEFF.   C. H. O.

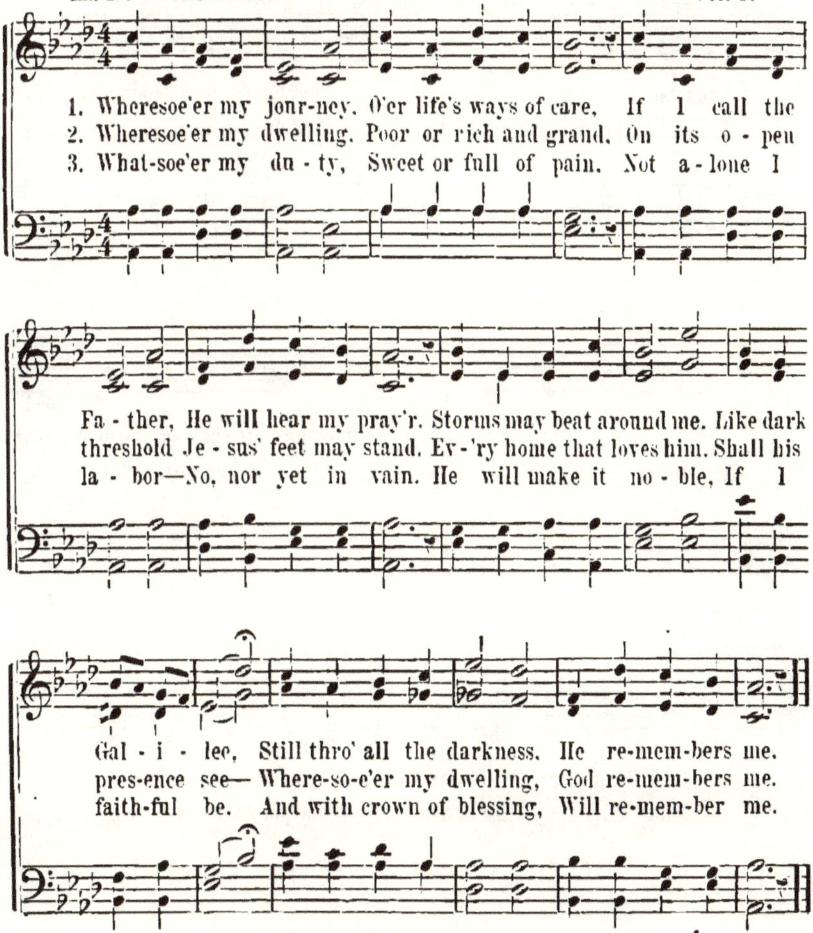

1. Wheresoe'er my journey, O'er life's ways of care, If I call the
2. Wheresoe'er my dwelling, Poor or rich and grand, On its o-pen
3. What-soe'er my du-ty, Sweet or full of pain, Not a-lone I

Fa-ther, He will hear my pray'r. Storms may beat around me. Like dark
threshold Je-sus' feet may stand. Ev-'ry home that loves him. Shall his
la-bor—No, nor yet in vain. He will make it no-ble, If I

Gal-i-lee, Still thro' all the darkness, He re-mem-bers me.
pres-ence see— Where-so-e'er my dwelling, God re-mem-bers me.
faith-ful be. And with crown of blessing, Will re-mem-ber me.

Copyright, 1888, by THE JOHN CHURCH CO.

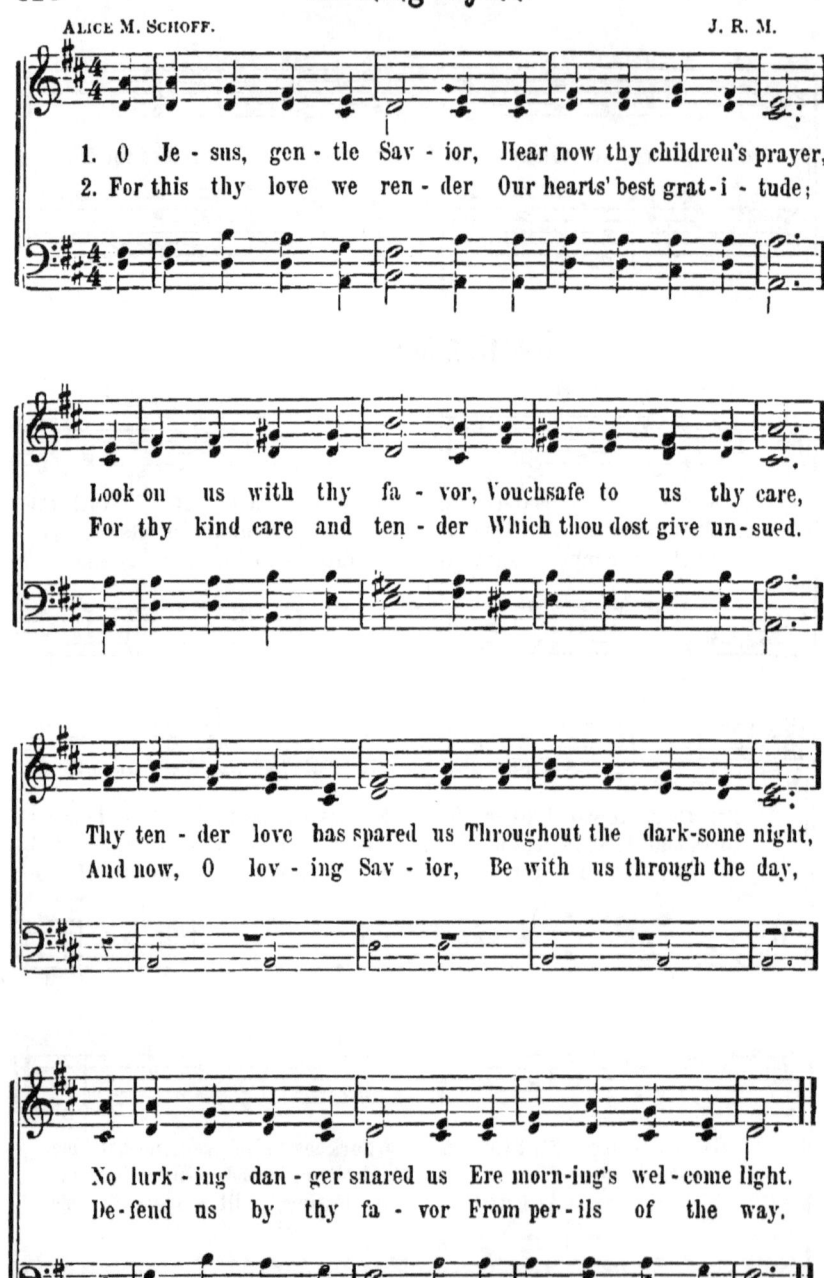

118. All the Way Home.

Mrs. E. W. Chapman.
May be sung as a Solo.
J. H. Tenney.

1. All the way home the Savior will guide you, Comfort, sustain, whatever betide you, He by his grace all your need will supply, Well-springs of love are abundant on high, Ever and ever his care will be nigh, All the way home, all the way home; Ever and ev-

2. All the way home his promise shall cheer you, In ev-'ry toil he'll surely be near you, Tenderly feed you with manna divine; Graciously teach you with line upon line, Ever and ever his mercy shall shine, All the way home, all the way home; Ever and ev-

3. All the way home the Savior will bless you, Fears all in vain shall seek to distress you, Brightly his light on your pathway shall gleam. Guiding your steps with its radiant beam. Ever and ever its brilliance shall stream, All the way home, all the way home; Ever and ev-

Copyright, 1887, by The John Church Co.

All the Way Home. 119

er his care will be nigh, All the way home, all the way home.
er his mer-cy shall shine, All the way home, all the way home.
er its brilliance shall stream, All the way home, all the way home.

Prayer.

Miss CLARA OGLESBY, by per

1. Rest this wea-ry heart, Blest Christ omnip-o-tent, Soothe this burning
2. Stay these burning tears, Changeless, omniscient Friend, Banish cru-el

smart Of mor-tal dis-con-tent. Shine thro' gloomy grief, Ex-
fears, My help-less-ness de-fend. Nerve for cease-less strife, Thou

haustless Source of Light, Send, oh, send relief From sorrow's painful blight.
con-quer-or di-vine, Sancti-fy this life, And seal it ev-er thine.

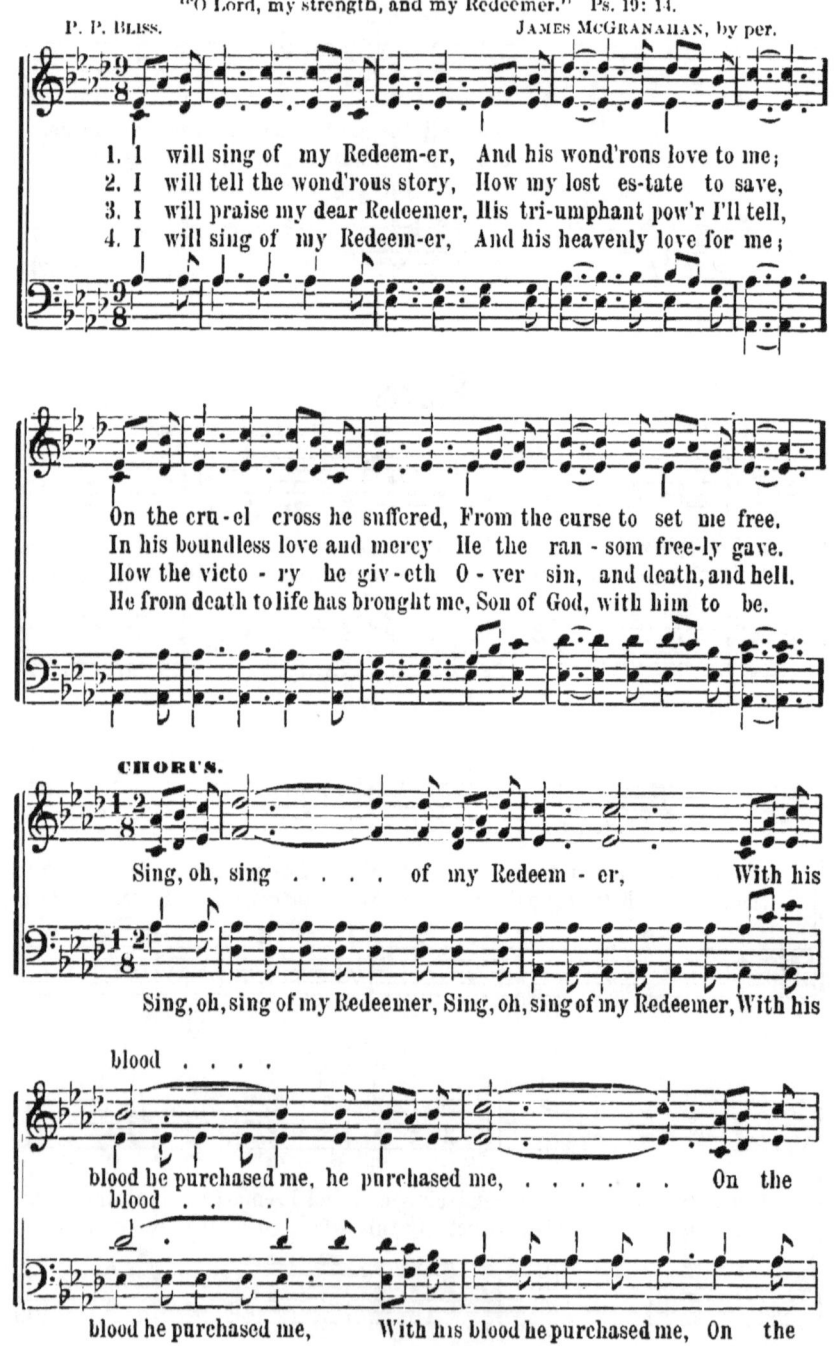

My Redeemer. 121

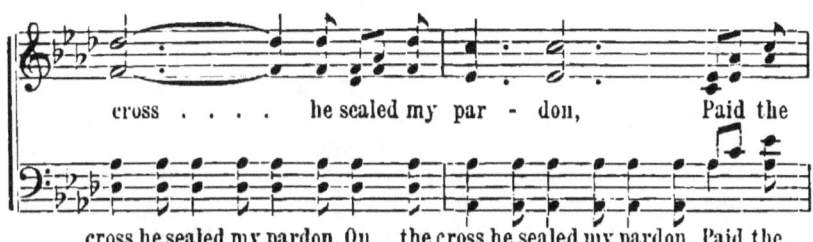

cross .... he sealed my par-don, Paid the
cross he sealed my pardon, On the cross he sealed my pardon, Paid the

Repeat *pp* after last verse.
free. . . . . . .
debt, ... and made me free, and made me free.
debt, and made me free, and made me free. . . . .

Dennis. S. M.

Rev. J. Fawcett, 1772.   From H. G. Naegeli.

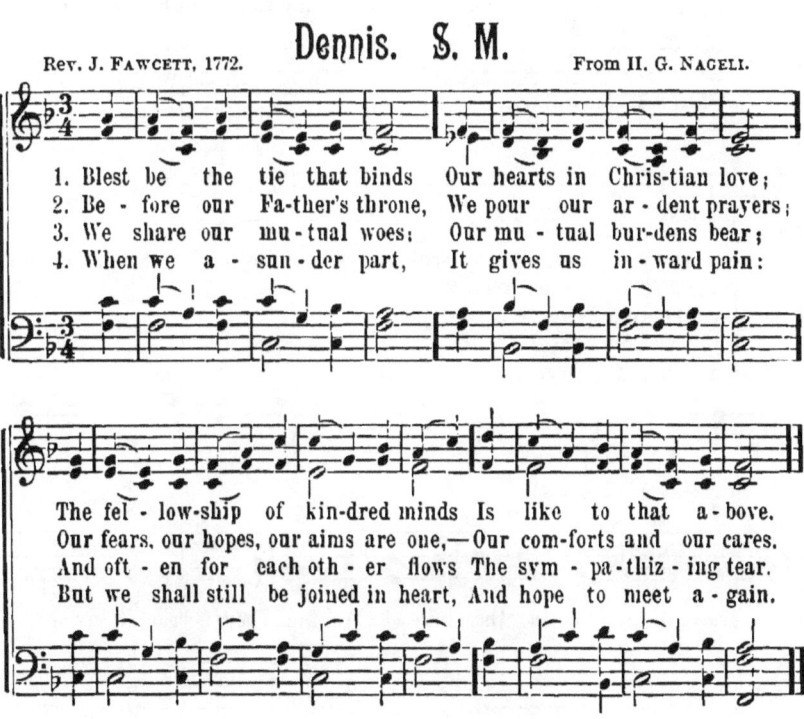

1. Blest be the tie that binds Our hearts in Chris-tian love;
2. Be-fore our Fa-ther's throne, We pour our ar-dent prayers;
3. We share our mu-tual woes; Our mu-tual bur-dens bear;
4. When we a-sun-der part, It gives us in-ward pain:

The fel-low-ship of kin-dred minds Is like to that a-bove.
Our fears, our hopes, our aims are one,—Our com-forts and our cares.
And oft-en for each oth-er flows The sym-pa-thiz-ing tear.
But we shall still be joined in heart, And hope to meet a-gain.

122. The Smile of the King.

Rev. Elias Nason.   A SONG OF ENCOURAGEMENT.   J. R. Murray.

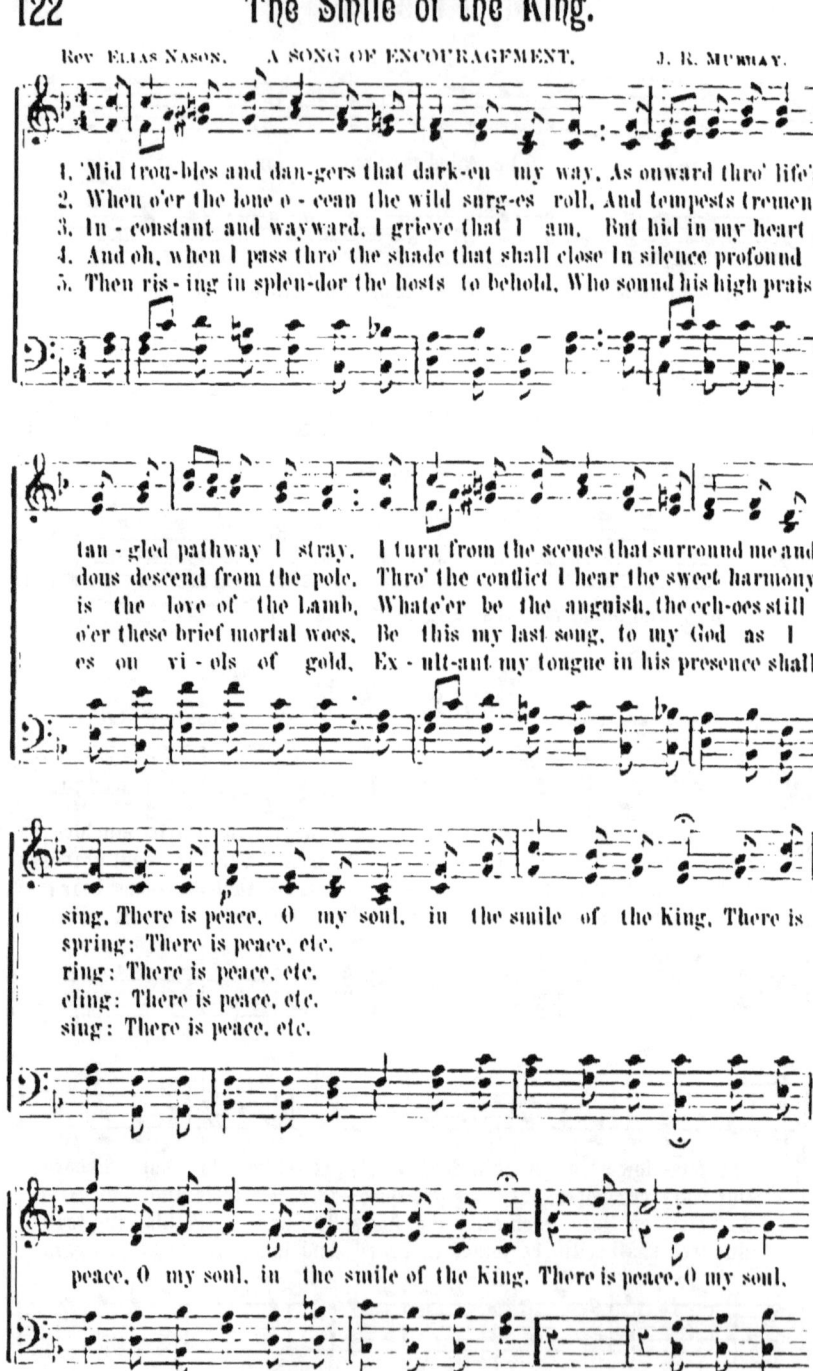

1. 'Mid troubles and dangers that darken my way, As onward thro' life's tangled pathway I stray, I turn from the scenes that surround me and sing, There is peace, O my soul, in the smile of the King, There is peace, O my soul, in the smile of the King, There is peace, O my soul.

2. When o'er the lone ocean the wild surges roll, And tempests tremendous descend from the pole, Thro' the conflict I hear the sweet harmony spring: There is peace, etc.

3. Inconstant and wayward, I grieve that I am, But hid in my heart is the love of the Lamb, Whate'er be the anguish, the echoes still ring: There is peace, etc.

4. And oh, when I pass thro' the shade that shall close In silence profound o'er these brief mortal woes, Be this my last song, to my God as I cling: There is peace, etc.

5. Then rising in splendor the hosts to behold, Who sound his high praises on viols of gold, Exultant my tongue in his presence shall sing: There is peace, etc.

Copyright, 1887, by The John Church Co.

The Smile of the King. 123

There is peace, O my soul, There is peace, O my soul, in the smile of the King.

The Cross and Crown.

AN ANNIVERSARY WORK SONG.

Arr. J. R. M.

1. The cross is for on-ly a day, The crown is for ev-er and aye;
2. The cross till the conflict is done, The crown when the vict'ry is won,
3. Then boldly the cross bear a-long, Our toil will give place soon to song,

The one for a night that will soon be gone, And one for e-ter-
A mo-ment 'tis on-ly for pain and strife, But thro' end-less ag-
When la-bor is ended, no more shall we roam, For Je-sus, our Sav-

ni-ty's glo-rious morn, And one for e-ter-ni-ty's glorious morn.
es the crown of life, But thro' endless ag-es the crown of life.
ior, will welcome us home, For Je-sus, our Savior, will welcome us home.

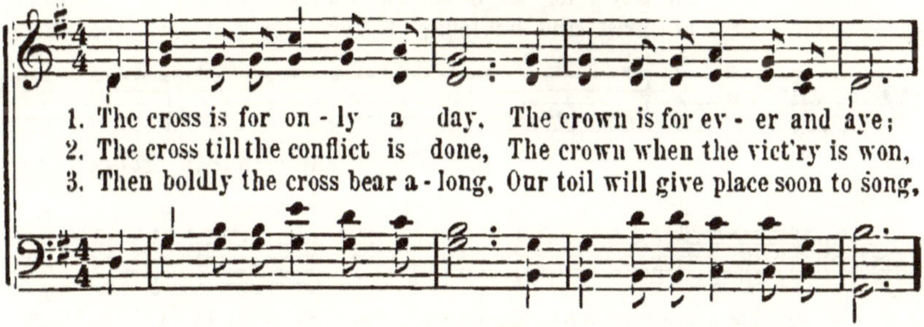

Copyright, 1887, by THE JOHN CHURCH CO.

The Light that Once in Judah Shone. 125

"He that believeth on the Son of God hath the witness in himself." 1 John 5 10.

H. BUTTERWORTH. By permission

1. The light that once in Ju-dah shone, We may no more behold;
   No bright She-ki-nah makes its throne 'Mid cher-u-bim of gold;
   No more the pen-te-cost-al flame Re-turns to ho-ly men,
   But God re-veals his grace the same To wait-ing souls as then.

2. My soul be-hold the end-less light In Je-sus' reign be-gin;
   The flame that once without was bright, Now shines more bright within;
   No long-er to the eye of sense The out-ward vis-ion glows,
   But in the in-ward ev-i-dence Doth Christ his love dis-close.

3. Yes, though his rays no lon-ger shine The gold-en ark a-bove,
   Within the spir-it's in-most shrine Still glows Im-man-uel's love;
   There dwells his glory as of yore—Then cease with doubt thy strife;
   In help-less darkness walk no more—Be-hold the Light of Life!

126. Follow the Light.

T. P. W.
THOS. P. WESTENDORF.

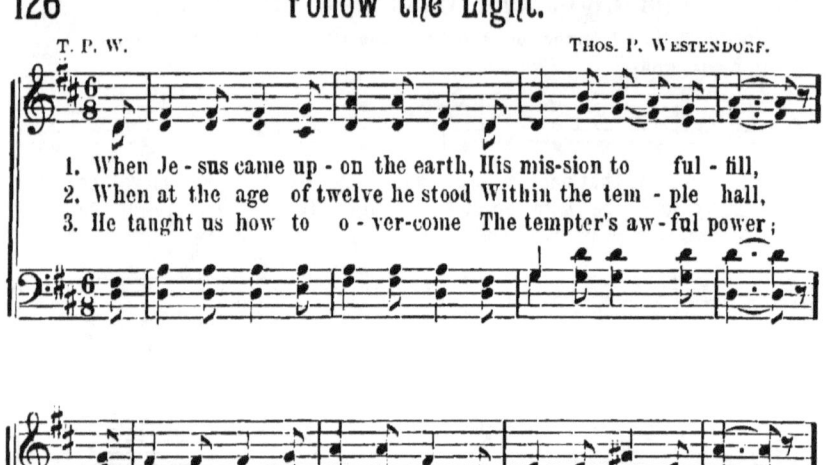

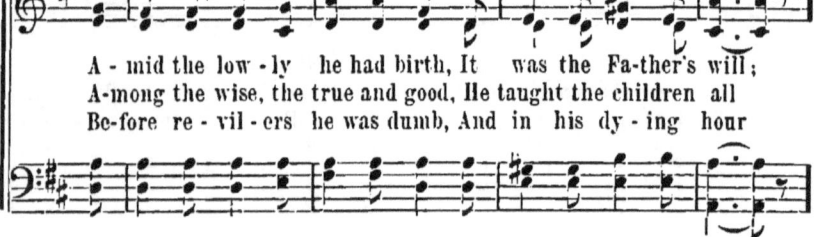

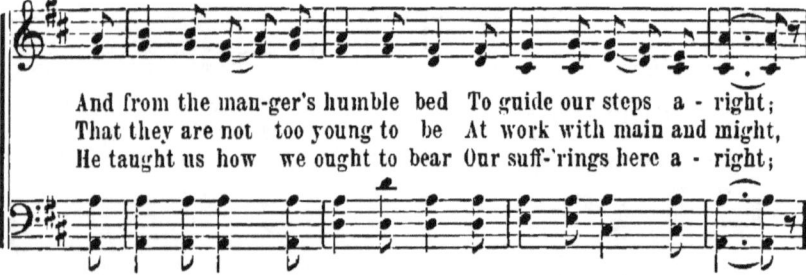

Copyright, 1888, by THE JOHN CHURCH Co.

Follow the Light.

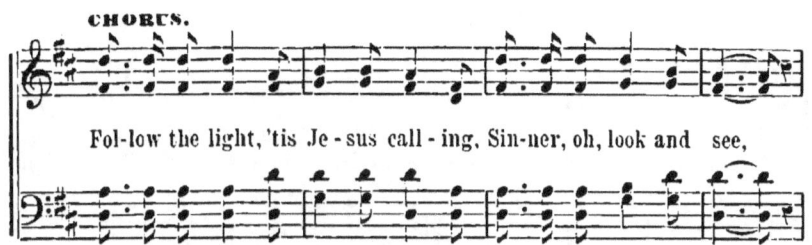

Gloria Patri.

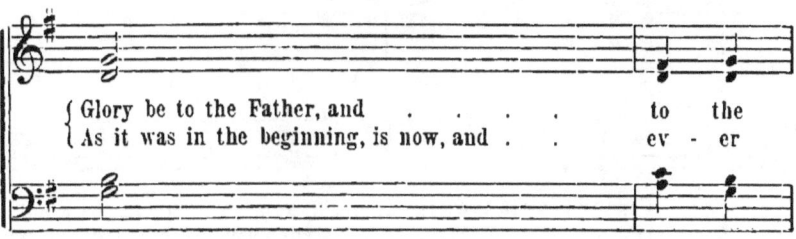

Lo! He Cometh.

Raise a song, a shout of triumph; On to battle for the Lord!

Is there Room for Me?

MARY E. BRADLEY.   K. W. BURT.

1. Lord, where thy many mansions be, Hast thou a little room for me?
2. Lord, if I heard, and in despite Of warning, chose the fair, false light,
3. Lord, is there an-y room for me, Who, sorrowing, would return to thee?

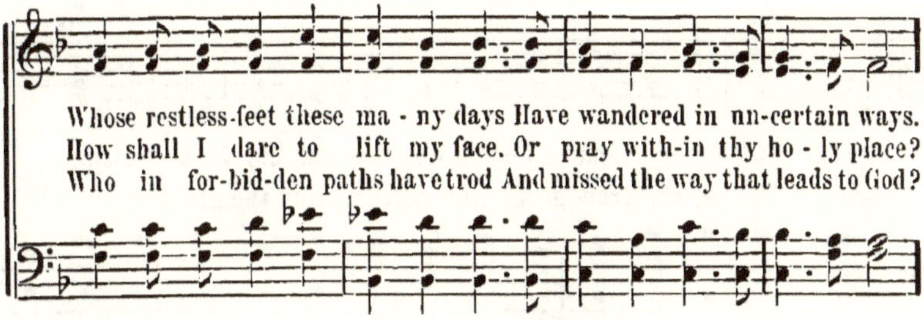

Whose restless feet these many days Have wandered in uncertain ways.
How shall I dare to lift my face, Or pray within thy holy place?
Who in forbidden paths have trod And missed the way that leads to God?

CHORUS.

I long to walk, O God, with thee, Lord, hast thou any room for me?

Copyright, 1888, by THE JOHN CHURCH CO.

130 Waiting for Jesus.

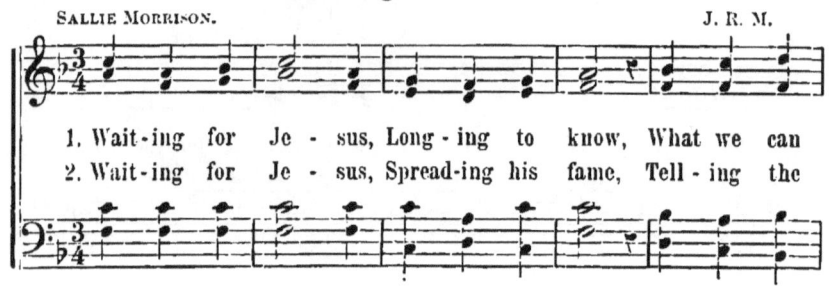
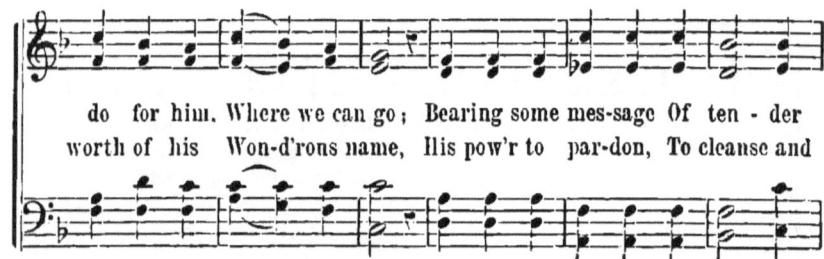

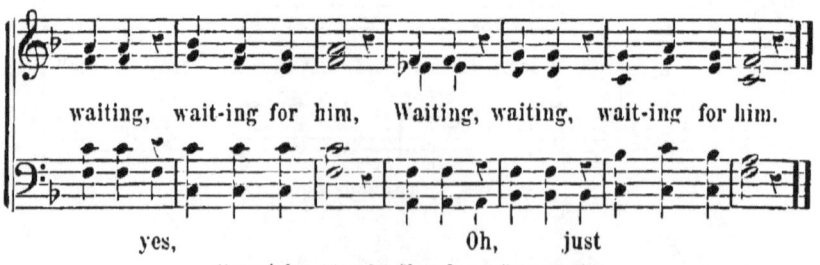

Copyright, 1888, by The John Church Co.

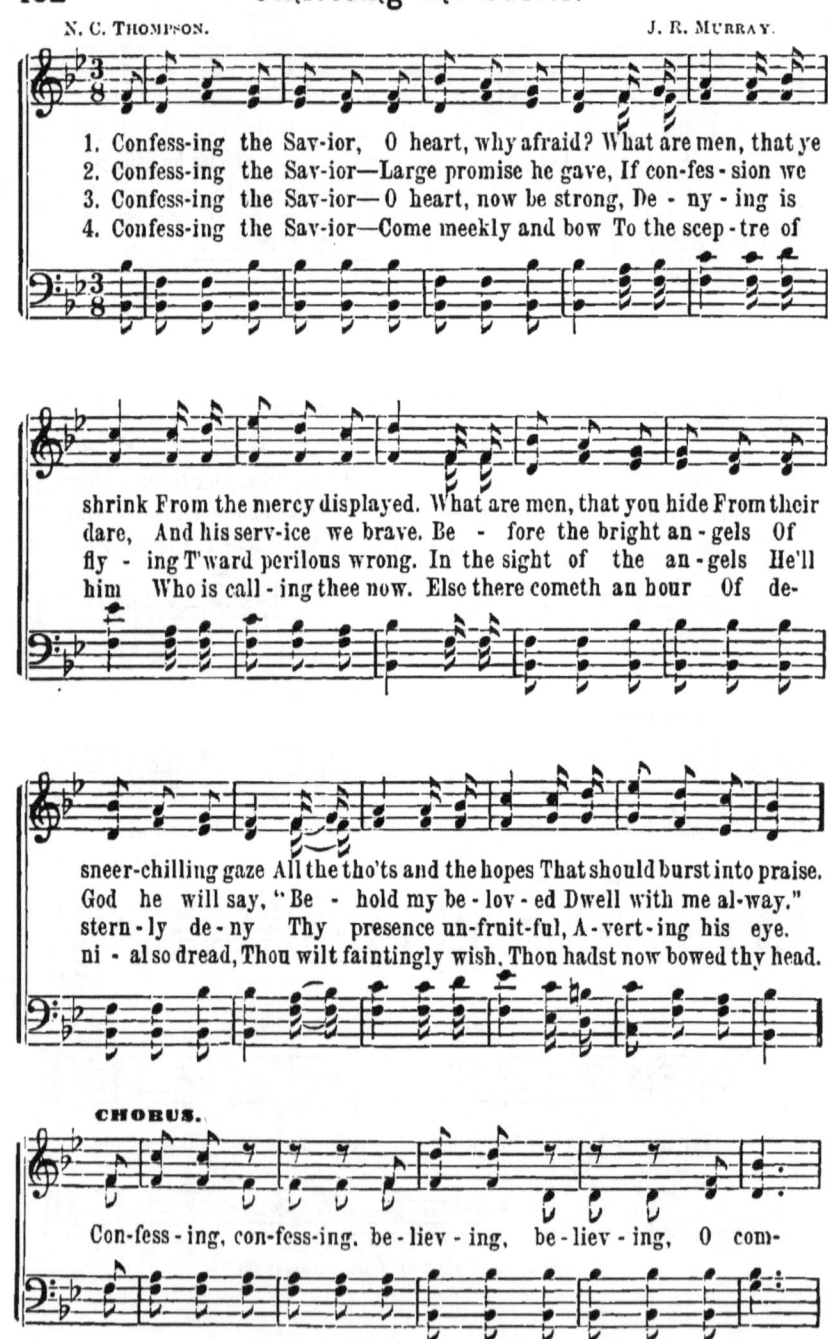

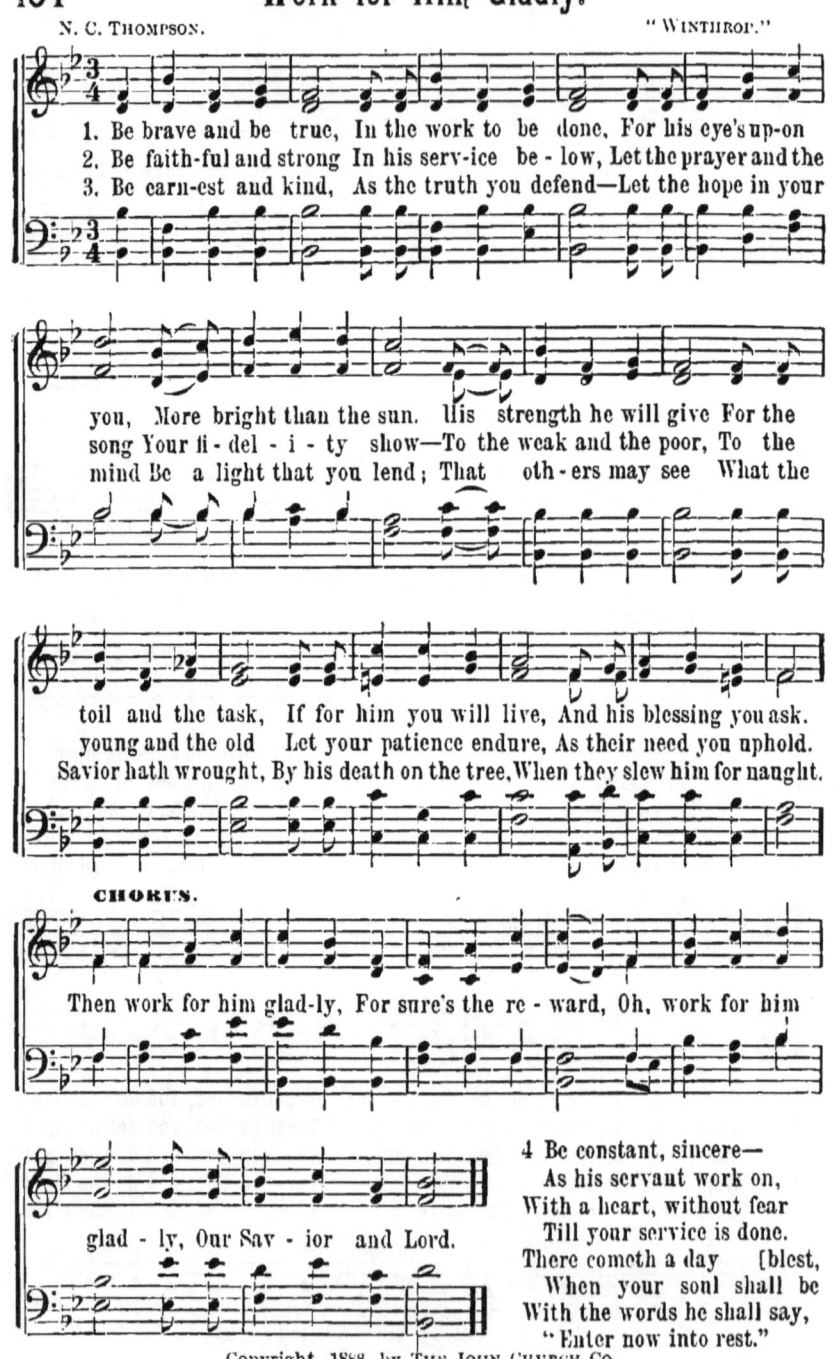

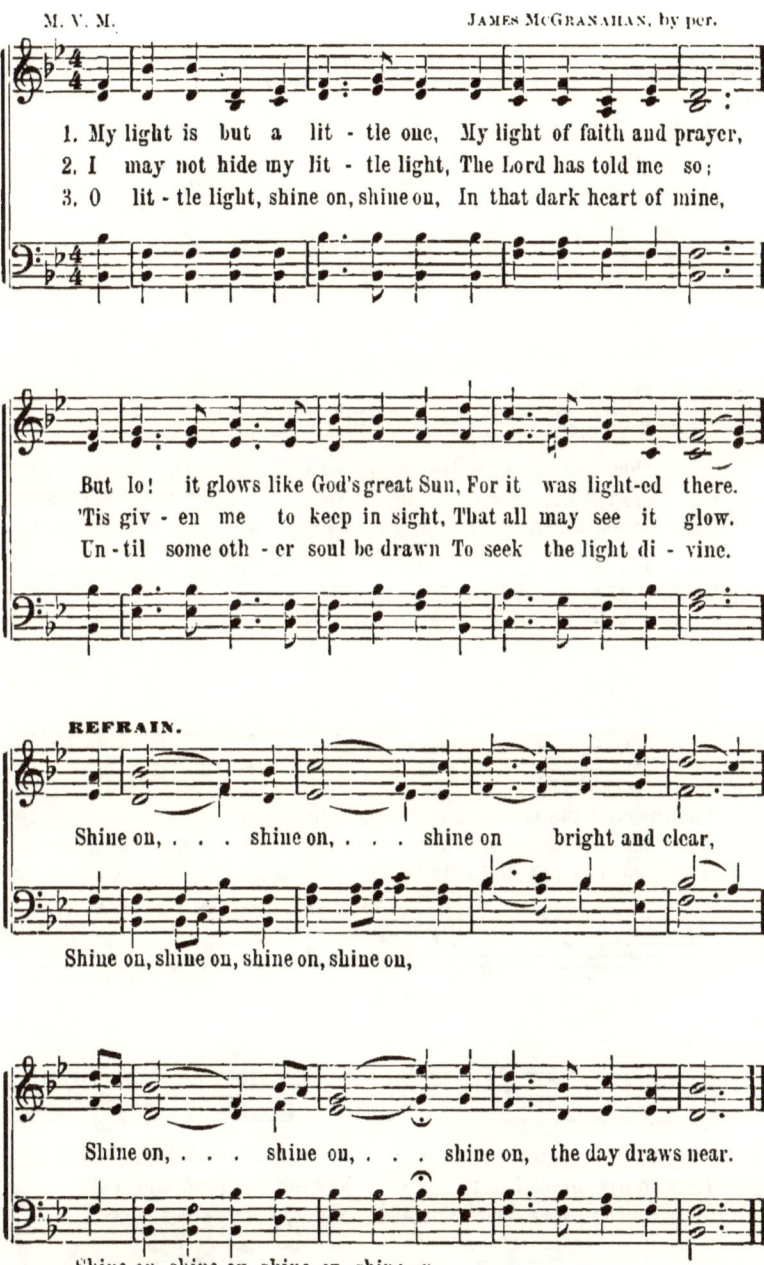

Close Up the Ranks. 137

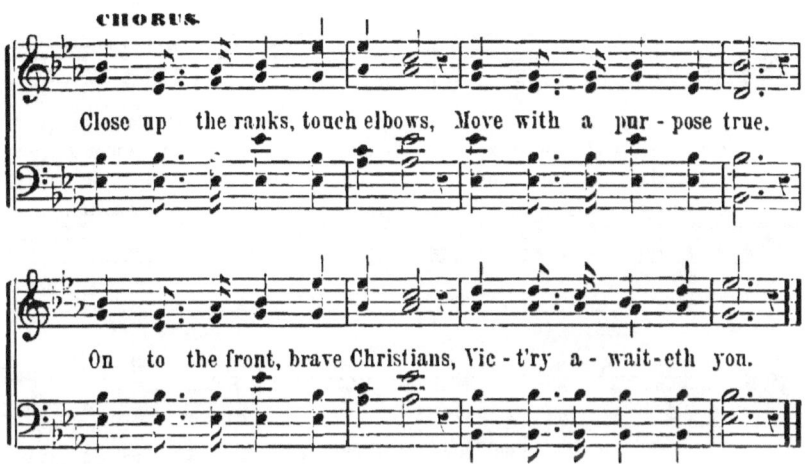

Close up the ranks, touch elbows, Move with a pur-pose true.
On to the front, brave Christians, Vic-t'ry a-wait-eth you.

DUKE STREET.

1 O Lord, our Guardian and our stay,
  Do thou our humble efforts bless,
And every evil take away,
  And spread the cause of righteousness.

2 From day to day thy power make
    known,
  Thy wisdom and thy truth divine;
And may we still thy goodness own,
  While round our path thy mercies
    shine.

3 The drunkard, Lord, in pity see,
  A slave to Satan and to sin;
Oh, teach him from all sin to flee;
  Restore and make him clean within.

TEMPERANCE.
By per.

1 Brothers! rally for the conflict,
  See the banner wave;
Temperance bands are passing onward,
  Fallen men to save.

CHORUS.
Hear a mighty host of freemen
  Songs of triumph raise;
Love hath conquered, chains are broken,
  Give to God the praise.

2 Burst the tyrants bands asunder,
    Set the captives free;
  Let rejoicing wives and mothers
    Shout the jubilee.
            WM. STEVENSON.

CLOSING HYMN.

1 Blessed Savior, watch us, guard us,
    As we leave our "Sabbath home;"
  Guide and keep us from all danger,
    Till again to thee we come.
  Though we very often wander,
    Sorely tempted, prone to sin,
  Yet we pray that thou wouldst hear us,
    Cleanse and make us pure within.

2 Make each spirit pure and lowly,
    Make us leave the ways of strife;
  Lead us in the path of duty,
    Lead us to the "better life."
  Thus we'd serve thee, blessed Savior,
    Till we've crossed life's stormy sea;
  And with each loved friend and teacher
    All are gathered home with thee.

The Little Missionary.

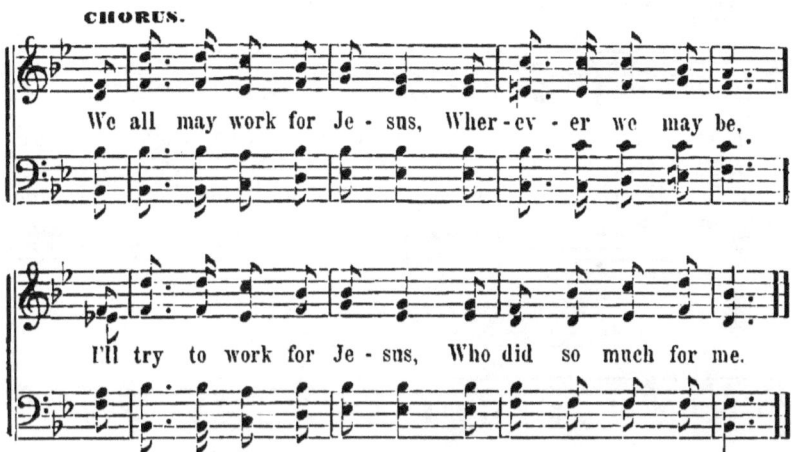

We all may work for Jesus, Wherever we may be,
I'll try to work for Jesus, Who did so much for me.

DEAR JESUS, EVER AT MY SIDE.

TUNE: "The Little Missionary," (omitting the chorus).

1 Dear Jesus, ever at my side,
   How loving must thou be
To leave thy home in heaven, to guard
   A little child like me.
Thy beautiful and shining face
   I see not, though so near;
The sweetness of thy soft, low voice
   I am too deaf to hear.

2 I can not feel thee touch my hand
   With pressure light and mild,
To check me as my mother did,
   When I was but a child.
But I have felt thee in my thoughts,
   Fighting with sin for me;
And when my heart loves God, I know
   The sweetness is from thee.

3 And when, dear Savior! I kneel down,
   Morning and night to prayer,
Something, there is, within my heart
   Which tells me Thou art there.
Yes! when I pray, thou prayest too—
   Thy prayer is all for me;
But when I sleep, thou sleepest not,
   But watchest patiently.

Rev. F. W. FABER.

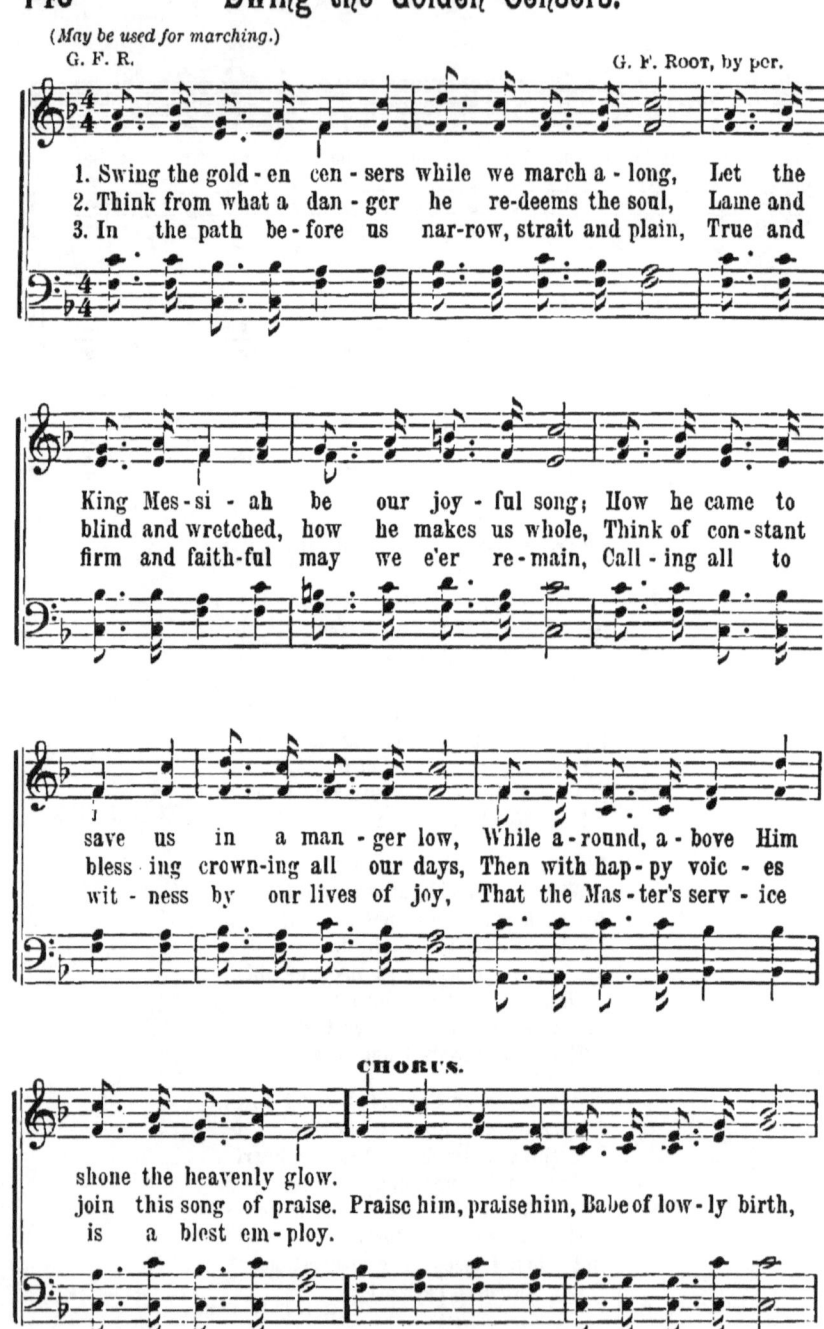

Swing the Golden Censers.

Lord, Thy Happy Children.

Words and music by J. R. M.

1. For Sabbath morning bright and fair, Lord, thy happy children praise thee;
2. For lov-ing deeds this day inspires, Lord, thy happy children praise thee;
3. For joy of earth and hope of heav'n, Lord, thy happy children praise thee;

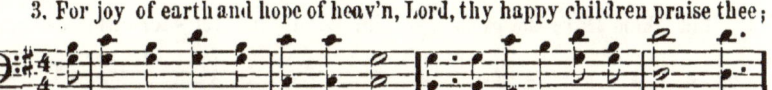

For all its treasures rich and rare, Lord, thy happy children praise thee.
For holy thoughts and good desires, Lord, thy happy children praise thee.
For all the blessings thou hast given, Lord, thy happy children praise thee.

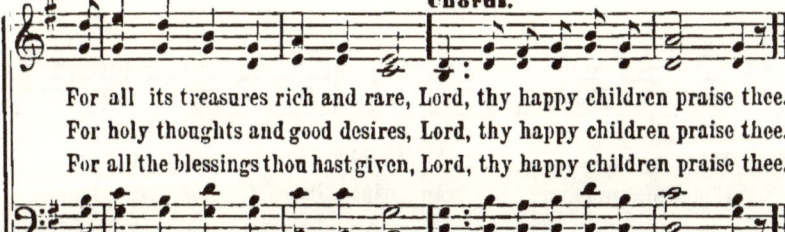

Copyright, 1888, by THE JOHN CHURCH CO.

142. Do It Now.

"WINTHROP."

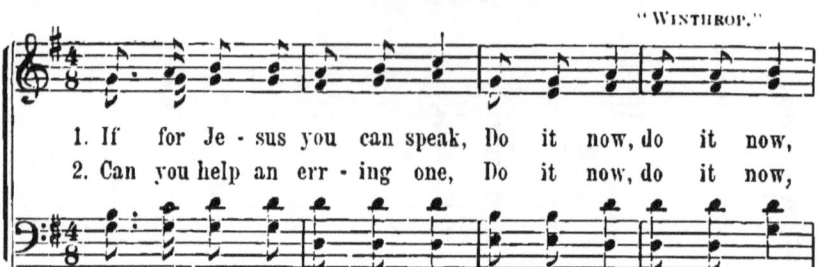

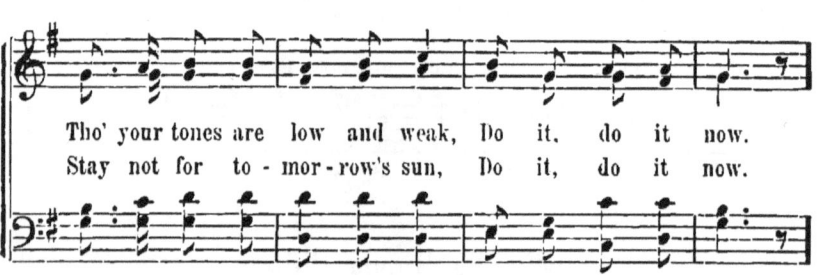

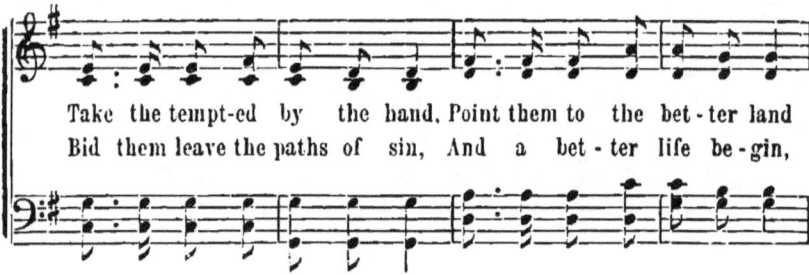

Copyright, 1888, by the John Church Co.

The Ten Virgins;
—OR—
When the Bridegroom Comes.

NOTE.—In the singing of the several verses let the tempo be governed by the sentiment to be expressed. Some of the words require a slower movement than others. The line, "Go ye out to meet him," should be sung very fast. The Chorus must be closely connected to each verse. The whole song should be sung without interludes. It is impossible to represent in notes the peculiar effects produced by the colored people, from whose singing this music was arranged. The singers can very easily adapt the words to the music.

J. R. MURRAY.

1. Five of them were wise when the Bridegroom came, Five of them were
2. Five of them were foolish when the Bridegroom came, Five of them were
3. The foolish had no oil when the Bridegroom came, The foolish had no
4. The foolish kept a-knocking when the Bridegroom came, The foolish kept a-

wise when the Bridegroom came, Five of them were wise,
foolish when the Bridegroom came, Five of them were foolish,
oil when the Bridegroom came, The fool-ish had no oil, The
knocking when the Bridegroom came, The foolish kept a-knocking, The

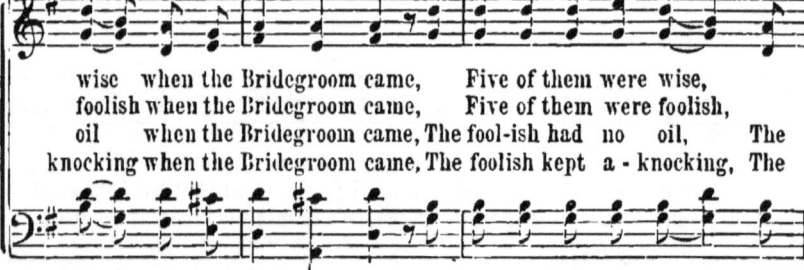

Five of them were wise, Five of them were wise when he came.
Five of them were foolish, Five of them were foolish when he came.
fool-ish had no oil, The fool-ish had no oil when he came.
fool-ish kept a knocking, The fool-ish kept a-knocking when he came.

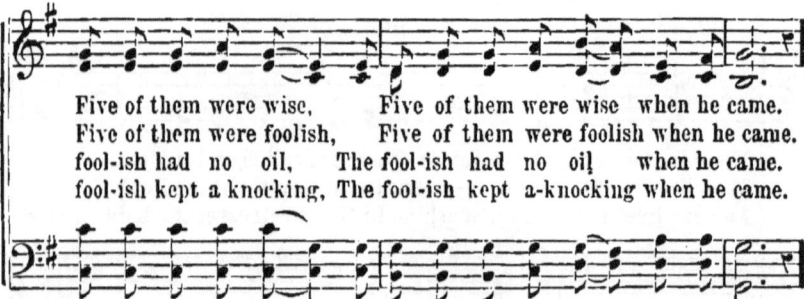

Copyright, 1888, by THE JOHN CHURCH CO.

The Ten Virgins.

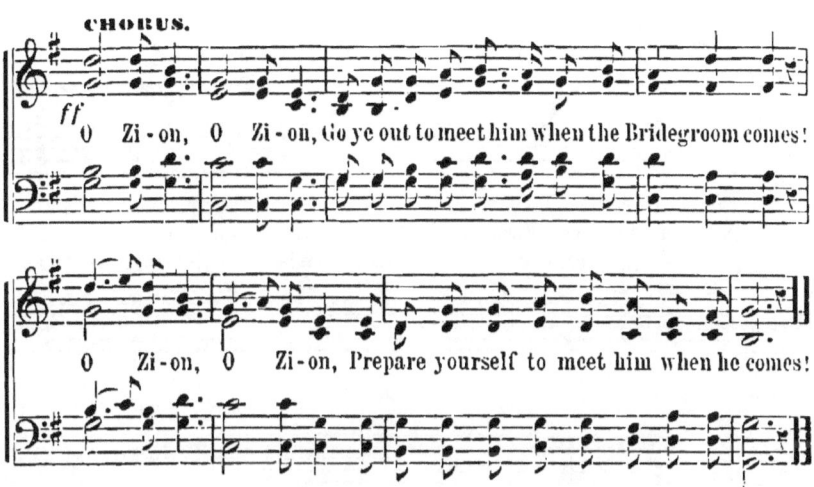

5 Go ye out to meet him, when the Bridegroom comes!
  Go ye out to meet him, when the Bridegroom comes!
  ‖: Go ye out to meet him, :‖ when he comes!

6 Have your lamps a-burning when the Bridegroom comes,
  Have your lamps a-burning when the Bridegroom comes,
  ‖: Have your lamps a-burning, :‖ when he comes.

Away all Anxious Sorrow.

T. K. L.   SCHNEIDER.

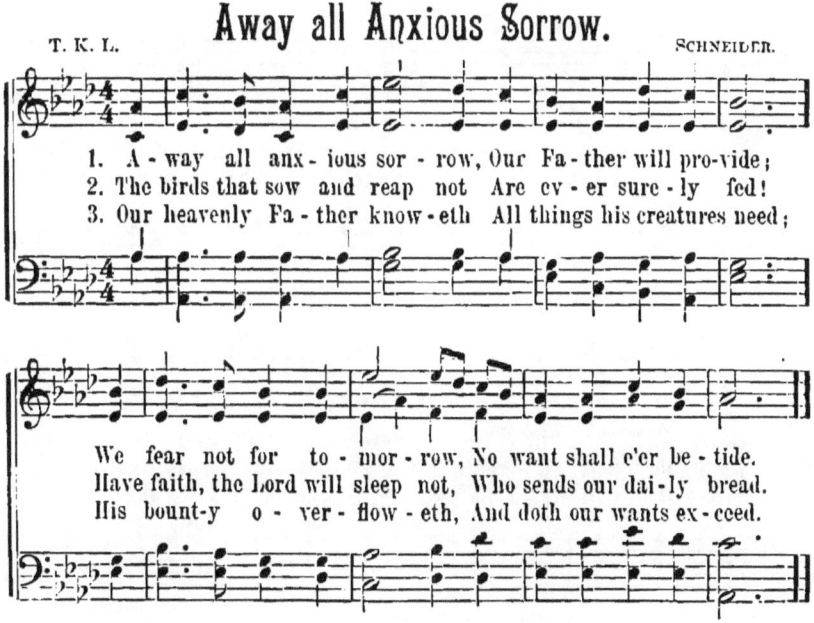

1. A-way all anx-ious sor-row, Our Fa-ther will pro-vide;
2. The birds that sow and reap not Are ev-er sure-ly fed!
3. Our heavenly Fa-ther know-eth All things his creatures need;

We fear not for to-mor-row, No want shall e'er be-tide.
Have faith, the Lord will sleep not, Who sends our dai-ly bread.
His boun-ty o-ver-flow-eth, And doth our wants ex-ceed.

Tekel.

4 Are you sure that you are honest?
  Have you ever told a lie?
Do you covet what your neighbor calls his own?
  Oh, consider now, my brother.
  That the soul that sins shall die;
By repentance you can only now atone.

148. Luther's Cradle Hymn.

(Composed by Martin Luther for his children, and still sung by German mothers to their little ones.)
Music by J. R. M.

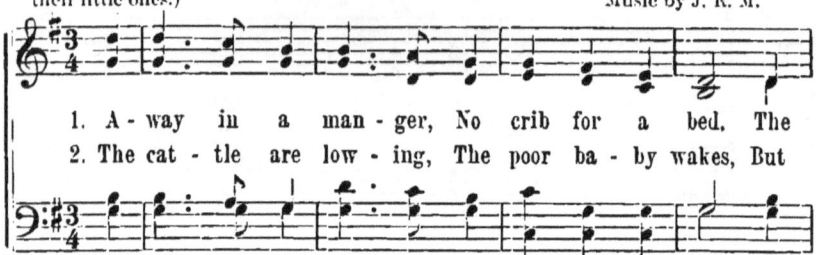
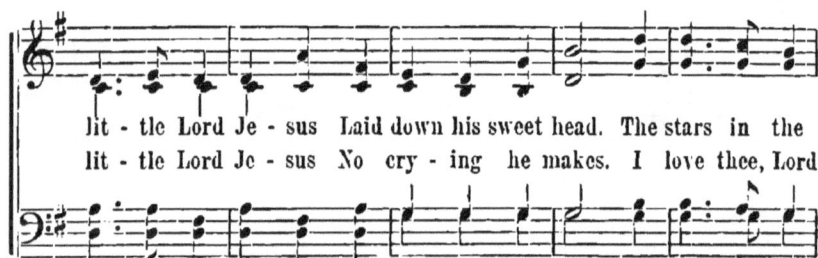

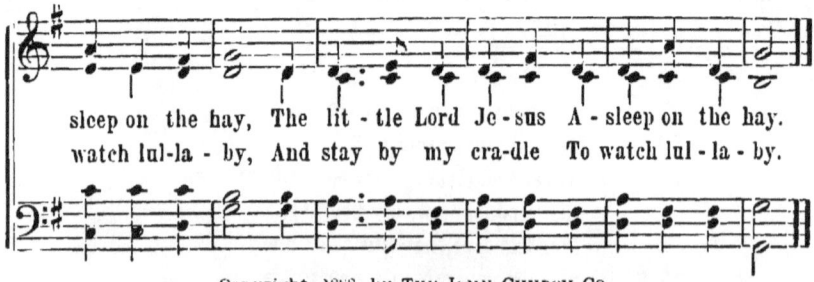

Copyright, 1888, by The John Church Co.

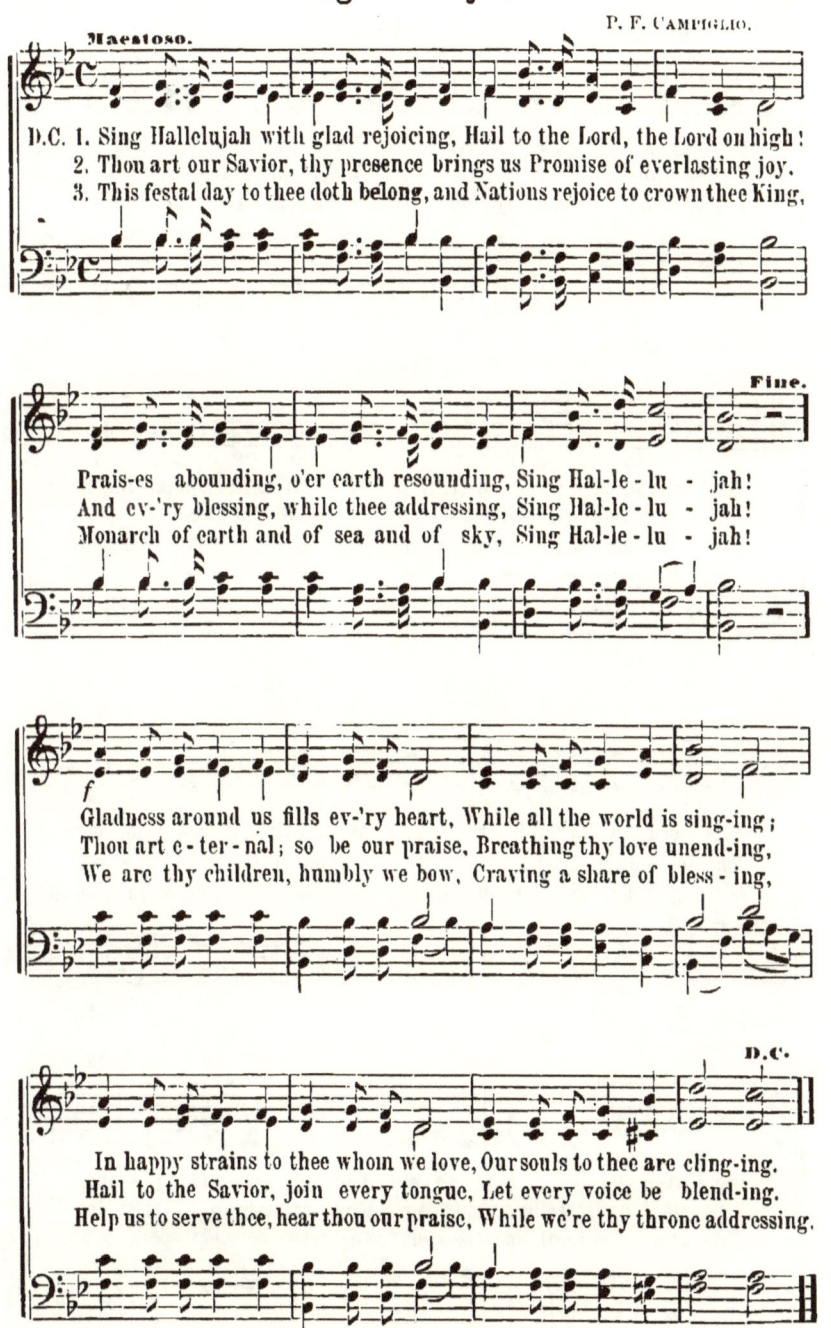

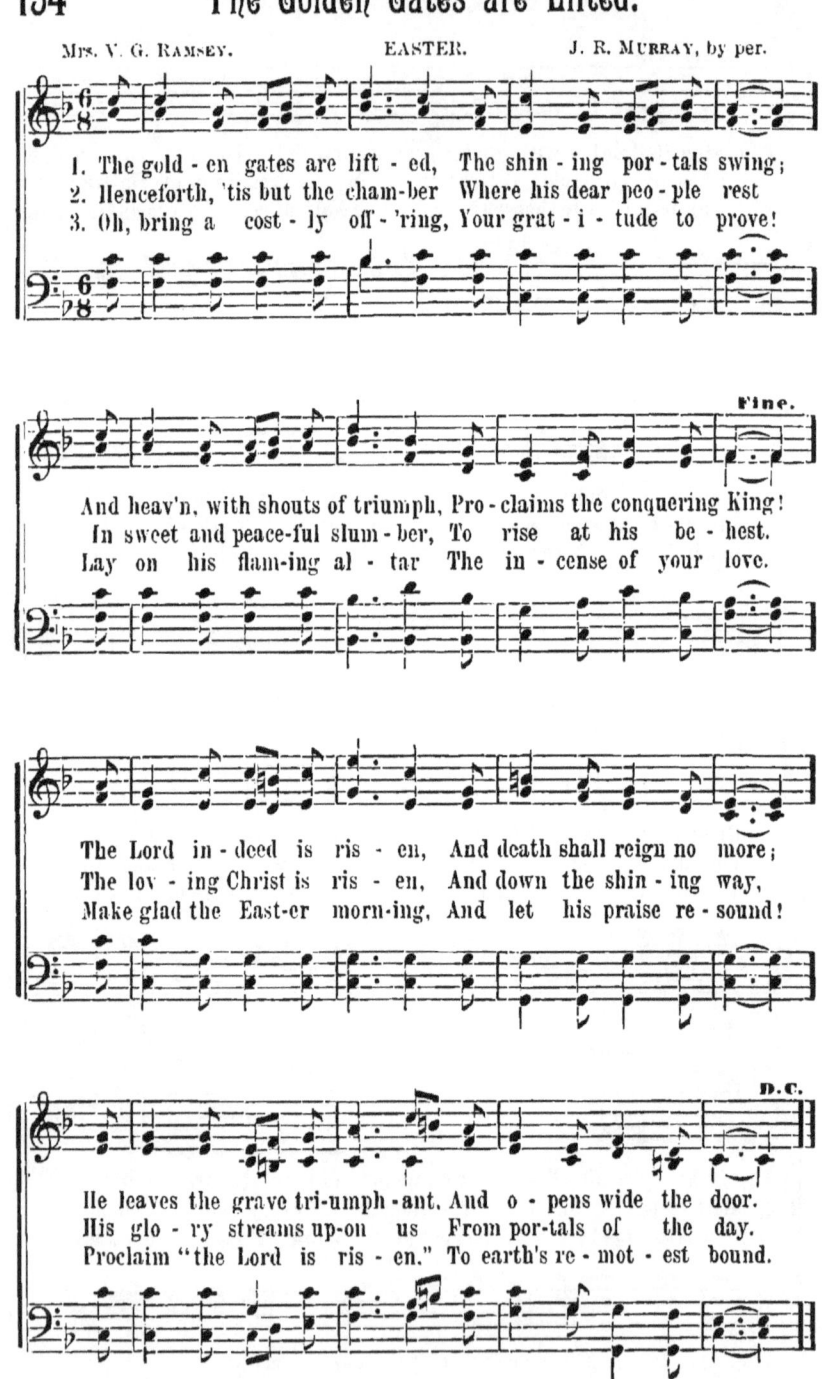

Once More We Gather. 155

FLOWER SUNDAY OR CHILDREN'S DAY.

CLARA LOUISE BURNHAM.   G. F. ROOT.

1. Once more we gath-er here, a hap-py band, Wel-come the day,
2. Blessings have crowned the work we've found to do, All thro' the year,
3. Now 'mid the song of birds and scent of flowers Meet we a-gain.

Wel-come the day; Once more to bless the kind protect-ing hand
All thro' the year, When we have sought the Master's will to know,
Meet we a-gain, Greeting the friends who bless our happiest hours,

CHORUS.

Which has brought us on our way.
And have felt his pres-ence near.   Joy-ful the prais-es that to
And the cause of right maintain.

heaven we send, Glad ev-'ry heart here to-day; For oh, in his

love, who is the sin-ner's Friend, We may re-joice al-way.

Copyright, 1887, by THE JOHN CHURCH CO.

156. O Holy Night.

ALICE M SCHOFF.   CHRISTMAS.   J. R. M

1. Come, let us all in joyful strain Sing of that wondrous night a-gain.
2. Now raise the song in glad accord, To praise the birth-night of our Lord,
3. Come, sing the song with joyful might, And marvel at that glorious night,

When low-ly lay and gen-tly smiled The bless-ed Sav-ior, meek and mild.
When trembling shepherds saw the sight Of heavenly brightness in the night.
When wise men, guided by a star, To wor-ship him came from a-far.

REFRAIN.

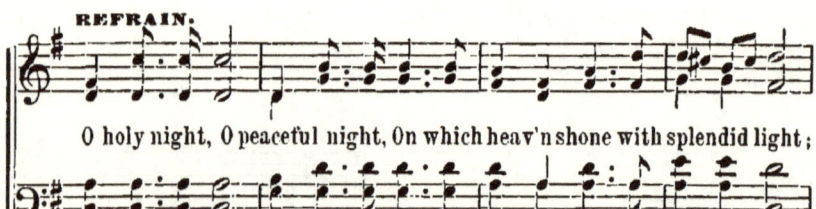

O holy night, O peaceful night, On which heav'n shone with splendid light;

O holy word, O gracious word, The waiting shepherds wond'ring heard.

Copyright, 1887, by THE JOHN CHURCH CO.

Teach Me, O Lord. 159

J. R. M.

Copyright, 1888, by The John Church Co.

ELEMENTS OF MUSIC.

LESSON I.

TONE, PROPERTIES, AND DEPARTMENTS.

1. A musical sound is called a *Tone*.
2. In every tone there is *length, pitch, power* and *quality*.
3. The *duration* of a tone is called length.
4. The *highness* or *lowness* of a tone is called its pitch.
5. The *loudness* or *softness* of a tone is called its power.
6. The *character* of a tone is called its quality.

NOTE.—The difference between a flute tone and a violin tone is a difference of quality. The same voice can make a joyful tone and a sad tone, a clear tone and a sombre tone; and these are differences, not of length, pitch or power, but of *quality*.

7. Length, pitch, power and quality are called the *properties* of tones.
8. *Rhythmics, Melodics, Dynamics* are the names of the *Departments* into which the science of music naturally divides itself.
9. Rhythmics treats of the length of sounds.
10. Melodics treats of the pitch of sounds.
11. Dynamics treats of the power and quality of sounds.
12. When people speak intelligently of the *rhythmic* character of a piece of music, they mean something about the tone-lengths used, or their accents, or the measure or movement in which they go.
13. When people speak of the *melodic* character of music, they mean something about the pitches used, their pleasant or peculiar succession, their highness or their lowness.
14. When people speak of the *dynamic* character of music, they mean something about the loudness or sweetness, or sadness or joyfulness of the tones, or both combined as loud and joyful, soft and sad, etc.

QUESTIONS.—What is a musical sound called? What is there in every tone? What is the duration of a tone called? the highness or lowness? the loudness or softness? Explain the term quality. What are length, pitch, power and quality called? Name the departments into which the science of music is divided. Of what does the first department treat? The second? The third? What is a tone? When people speak of the melodic character of music, to what do they refer? What is meant when speaking of Dynamics? Rhythmics?

LESSON II.

NOTES, BEATS AND MEASURES. RESTS.

1. The length or duration of tones is represented to the eye by characters called *notes*.

2. The names of notes, their shape and relative value are as follows:

The Whole Note,

which equals two Halves,

or four Quarters,

or eight Eighths,

or sixteen Sixteenths,

or thirtytwo Thirty-seconds.

3. Music is divided by *pulsations*, or *beats*, into small portions, called *measures*.

4. Measures are represented to the eye by the spaces between vertical lines, as follows:

| Measure | Measure | Measure | Measure ||

5. The vertical lines are called *bars*. The last one in the example above is called a *double bar*, or *close*.

6. There are various kinds of measures.

7. When the measures consist of two beats each, the music is said to be in *Double measure*.

8. A downward motion of the hand goes with the first beat in each measure, and an upward motion with the second beat in the measure. This is called *keeping*, or *beating time*. The first beat in a measure is always a strong or accented one.

9. A measure which has three beats is called *Triple measure*. The motions of the hand are *down, left, up*. The first beat is accented.

10. *Quadruple measure* has four beats. The motions of the hand are *down, left, right, up*. The first and third beats are accented in quadruple measure.

11. *Sextuple measure* has six beats with the motions *down, down, left, right, up, up*. The first and fourth beats are accented.

12. The kind of measure together with the number and kind of notes taken as the unit or beat-note are represented by figures in the form of a

fraction. Any kind of a note or rest, equivalent in value to that indicated by the figure, may appear in a measure.

13. The upper figure of the fraction indicates the *kind* of measure, and the lower one the kind of note taken as the unit or beat-note. For example, Double measure, with the quarter note as the beat-note, is indicated thus, $\frac{2}{4}$ Triple measure, $\frac{3}{4}$ Quadruple measure, $\frac{4}{4}$ etc.

14. *Rests* are signs indicating silence. Each note has its corresponding rest. Their names and shapes are as follows:

Whole rest.	Half rest.	Quarter.	Eighth.	Sixteenth.	Thirty-second.

QUESTIONS.—How is the length of tones represented? Give the names of the notes and their relative value. Into what is music divided by pulsations or beats? How are measures represented to the eye? What are the vertical lines called? What are the two heavy ones called? Is there more than one kind of measure? Name the measure that has two beats? What is beating time? What are the hand motions for double measure? What can you say of the first beat of every measure? Name the measure that has three beats. What are the hand motions? Which beat is accented? Name the measure that has four beats. What are the motions? Which beats are accented? Name the measure which has six beats. What are the motions? Which beats are accented? What do fraction figures represent? What does the upper figure indicate? What the lower one? What figure represents double measure? Triple measure? Quadruple measure? Sextuple measure? If a measure consists of three beats with the quarter note as the beat-note, what kind of measure is it, and how would it be represented by figures? What are rests? Name and describe them.

LESSON III.

DOTTED NOTES AND RESTS.

1. Notes and rests may be made to indicate longer lengths by the addition of dots.

2. A dot placed after a note or rest increases its value one-half. For example: A whole note equals two half notes; a dot added to it, thus, ○· makes it the equal of three half notes. A half note equals two quarters; a dot added to it makes it the equal of three quarters, etc. A quarter rest equals two eighths; a dot added to it, thus, ⸰ · makes it the equal of three eighths.

ILLUSTRATION.

Dotted whole	Dotted half	Dotted quarter	Dotted eighth
○·	♩.	♪.	♬.
equals	equals	equals	equals

3. Notes and rests may be double dotted. A second dot adds one-half of the value of the first dot, thus:

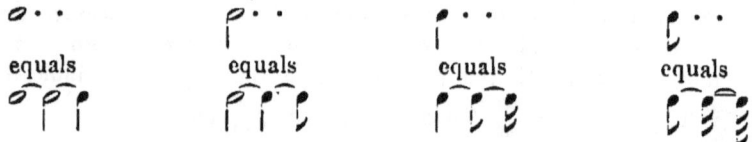

QUESTIONS.—How may notes and rests be made to indicate longer lengths? How many quarters does a dotted half equal? If a quarter rest is dotted, how much longer does the dot make it? When notes and rests are double dotted, how much does the second dot add to the length? Give an example.

LESSON IV.

VARIETIES OF MEASURE.

1. Any kind of a note may be taken as the unit, or beat-note.

2. The upper figure of the fraction, as before stated, indicates the *kind* of measure, and the lower one the kind of note taken as the beat-note. Thus in Triple measure with quarter notes as units the time-figure would be 3/4 ♩ ♩ ♩. With eighth notes as units the marking would be 3/8 ♪ ♪ ♪

EXAMPLE OF DIFFERENT KINDS OF MEASURE.

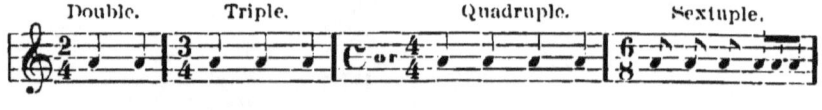

QUESTIONS.—May any kind of note be taken as beat-note? Explain the time-figure? With quarters as units or beat-notes, how would triple measure be marked? Quadruple with eighths? etc.

LESSON V.

PITCH, STAFF AND CLEFS.

1. The highness or lowness of a tone is called its *pitch*.

2. Tone-pitches are named with the names of certain letters, viz.: A, B, C, D, E, F, G.

3. The pitch of tones is represented by a character, called the *staff*. It consists, usually, of five horizontal lines and their spaces.

THE STAFF.

4. The lines and spaces of the staff are called *degrees*.

5. The exact pitch representation of the staff is fixed by characters called *clefs*.

6. There are two clefs in common use. The Soprano (or Treble), or G clef , and the Base, or F clef . In vocal music, in America, the C clef is sometimes used to indicate the Tenor part.

7. The G clef is always placed upon the second line of the staff, which is thus made to represent the pitch G, and all other pitches relatively, thus:

8. A staff with this clef upon it is called the Treble, or Soprano staff.

9. In piano or organ music the part for the right hand is written on the treble staff. So also the music for violin, flute, cornets, and other instruments of a similar character.

10. In vocal music the parts for women's voices, and sometimes the Tenor part, are written on the treble staff.

11. The F, or Base clef, is always placed upon the fourth line of the staff, thus indicating the pitch F.

12. The Bass staff is used for the left hand notes in piano or organ playing, and for the notes for men's voices, and represents pitches an octave, or eight notes, lower than does the treble staff and clef.

13. The C or Tenor clef is placed upon the third space of the staff in American vocal music.

14. The tenor and treble staffs read exactly alike, but the former represents pitches an octave lower than does the latter.

15. When other pitches are wanted, higher or lower than are represented by the staff, short lines called *added* or *leger lines* are used.

ADDED LINES.

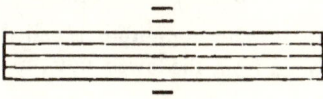

16. The base and treble staffs together, as in piano music, indicate the following pitches:

Middle C.

17. It will be observed that *Middle C* is common to both staffs, being represented by the added line above the base staff, which is the same thing in effect, as the added line below the treble staff.

18. The character which connects the two staffs at the left of the clefs is called a *brace* {.

QUESTIONS.—What is the name of the department which treats of pitch? What is meant by pitch? What are the pitch names of tones? How is the pitch of tones represented? What are degrees? Name and define the uses of the three clefs. What is that staff called which has the G clef upon it? That with the F clef? What pitch is represented by the second line of the treble staff? The second space? etc. Upon what line of the staff is the base clef placed? What pitch is represented by it? What can you say about the use of these staffs for piano or organ playing? How do the tenor and treble staffs differ from each other? How are pitches represented which are not indicated by the regular staff? What is that character called which is used to connect the staffs?

LESSON VI.

KEYS, SCALES AND INTERVALS.

1. A *key* is a group or family of tones closely related to each other.

2. Tone one, the principle or foundation tone of the key, is called the *key-note* or *key-tone*.

3. A *scale* is the tones of a key in a certain order, viz.: 1, 2, 3, 4, 5, 6, 7, 8.

4. There are but seven different tones in a key. The tone eight, which is always included in a complete scale, is but the tone one of the same key and scale an octave higher.

5. That key which consists of the tones C, D, E, F, G, A, B, is called the key of C, and when arranged in the order given above, make what is called the scale of C. It is represented upon the staff thus:

6. The distance from one tone to another is called an *interval*.

7. Intervals are reckoned from the lowest note upward, counting the first and last.

ELEMENTS OF MUSIC. 167

8. The musical effect of the smallest interval is called a *second*. There are *two* kinds of seconds, large and small, or *Major* and *Minor*.

9. A major second consists of two tones the distance from the first to the second of which is called (for the sake of measurement) a *step*, as from C to D.

10. A minor second consists of two tones the distance from the first to the second of which is called a *half-step*, as from E to F.

11. In Major Diatonic scales (the key of C, represented on previous page, is one) these half-steps occur between three and four, and seven and eight.

12. Here is the C scale, showing the steps and half-steps.

N.B.—Singers need not be troubled about these intervals; they are natural ones, and one at all musical can not help singing them correctly. We speak of them as a matter of theory.

QUESTIONS.—What is a key? What is tone one called? Why? What is a scale? How many different tones in a key? How many are necessary to form a complete scale? Name the tones which compose the key of C. What is an interval? How are they reckoned? What is the musical effect of the smallest interval called? How many kinds of seconds are they? What are there names? Of what does a major second consist? A minor second? Name an interval which forms a major second. Where do the half-steps occur in major diatonic scales?

LESSON VII.
INTERVALS CONTINUED.

1. There are other intervals than those mentioned in the preceding lesson. They take their names from the *name of the distance between the two tones*. For example: from any given tone of a key or degree of the staff to the third from it is called the interval of a *third*. From any tone to one a fourth from it is called a *fourth*. Tones five degrees apart make the interval of the *fifth*. Six degrees apart, a *sixth*. Seven degrees apart, a *seventh*. Eight degrees apart, an *octave*.

2. There are also major and minor thirds, sixths and sevenths.

3. A major third is as great as two steps, as from C to E.

4. A minor third consists of a step and a half-step, as from D to F.

5. A major sixth consists of four steps and a half-step, as from G to E.

6. A Minor sixth has three steps and two half-steps, as from E to C.

7. A major seventh contains five steps ane one half step, as from C to B.

8. A minor seventh contains four steps and two half-steps, as from D to C.

9. Fourths and Fifths are either Perfect, Augmented or Diminished.
10. A perfect fourth contains two steps and one half-step, as from C to F.

11. An augmented fourth contains three steps, as from F to B.

12. A diminished fourth contains one step and two half-steps.
13. A perfect fifth contains three steps and one half-step, as from C to G.

14. A diminished fifth contains two steps and two half-steps, as from B to F.

15. An augmented fifth contains four steps.

QUESTION.—Name the other intervals of the key. How many kinds of thirds are there? What are they? Of what does a major third consist? A minor third? A major sixth? A minor sixth? What is the difference between a major and minor seventh? What can you say of fourths and fifths? How many steps and half-steps has a perfect fourth? An augmented fourth? A diminished fourth? A perfect fifth? A diminished fifth? An augmented fifth?

LESSON VIII.

THE SHARP, FLAT AND NATURAL. INTERMEDIATE TONES.

1. The *Sharp, Flat* and *Natural* are used to modify the staff and cause it to represent other pitches, higher or lower, than those already indicated.

ELEMENTS OF MUSIC.

2. Between the regular tones of a key are other tones, called *intermediate tones.*

3. These intermediate tones are represented upon the staff by the use of the signs named above.

4. The *sharp* (♯) placed upon a line or space of the staff indicates a pitch a half-step higher, than is indicated without it. Thus in this example the second line in the first measure indicates the pitch G. In the second measure the meaning of the line is changed by placing a sharp upon it, and a pitch a half-step higher then G, between G and A is indicated, to which is given the name G-sharp.

5. The *flat* (♭) modifies the degree upon which it is placed and causes it to represent a tone a half-step lower than before. Thus the third line in the first measure indicates the pitch B. In the second measure the flat causes the line to indicate a pitch a half-step lower than B, between A and B, called B-flat.

6. The Natural (♮) is never used except upon a degree that has a sharp or flat upon it, and is used to change the degree back to its original significance.

EXAMPLE.

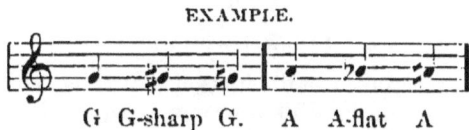

G   G-sharp   G.   A   A-flat   A

7. Sharps, flats and naturals occuring in the course of a piece of music are called *accidentals.*

8. Accidentals affect only the measure in which they are written.

9. Sharps and flats placed at the beginning of a piece of music, just after the clefs, affect the degrees upon which they are placed *throughout* the composition, unless modified by accidentals as above, and are called the *signature* or *sign of the key.*

20. The rules of Harmony often require the use of two other signs, called the *double sharp* (𝄪), and the *double flat* (𝄫). These signs are always placed upon degrees that have been "sharped," or "flatted," (that is, had sharps or flats placed upon them), and indicate tones a half-step higher, or lower than before, as will be seen from the following example.

G,   G-sharp,   G double sharp.   B,   B-flat, B double flat.

6. The intermediate tones of a key are called chromatic tones, and with the regular tones of a key, which are called diatonic tones, make what is called the chromatic scale.

Ascending.

Pitch names.	C,	C♯,	D,	D♯,	E,	F,	F♯,	G,	G♯,	A,	A♯,	B,	C.
Numeral names.	1,	sharp 1,	2,	sharp 2,	3,	4,	sharp 4,	5,	sharp 5,	6,	sharp 6,	7,	8.
Syllable names.	Do,	di,	re,	ri,	mi,	fa,	fi,	sol,	si,	la,	li,	ti,	do.

Descending.

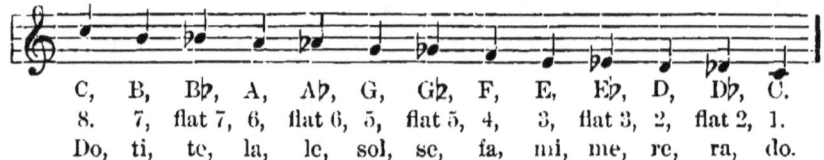

	C,	B,	B♭,	A,	A♭,	G,	G♭,	F,	E,	E♭,	D,	D♭,	C.
	8.	7,	flat 7,	6,	flat 6,	5,	flat 5,	4,	3,	flat 3,	2,	flat 2,	1.
	Do,	ti,	te,	la,	le,	sol,	se,	fa,	mi,	me,	re,	ra,	do.

QUESTIONS.—Define the use of the sharp, flat and natural. What are intermediate tones? How are they represented upon the staff? How does the sharp modify the staff? The flat? The natural? What are accidentals? What is meant by the signature or sign of the key? How far does the influence of an accidental extend? How do sharps or flats in the signature place effect the staff? What can you say of the double sharp and double flat? What are chromatic tones? What are the regular tones of the key called? What is meant by the chromatic scale?

LESSON IX.

KEYS WITH SHARPS.

1. Any tone may be taken as the basis of a key, but all major keys must have the same order and kind of intervals as shown in the scale of C, in Lesson IV. That is, the half-steps must come between 3 and 4, and 7 and 8.

2. The key of C is the only one in which the proper order of intervals can be represented without the use of sharps or flats. This is one reason why the key of C is often called the "natural key," but it is no more *natural* than any other.

3. In forming new keys the common method is to take the fifth of the preceding key for the first of the new one. The fifth of the key of C is G. A series of tones in scale form, with G as one, will appear as follows:

G	A	B	C	D	E	F	G
1	2	3	4	5	6	7	8

The half-steps are indicated by the curved lines, and, as will be readily seen, the second one does not come in the right place according to the rule, viz., between 7 and 8, but between 6 and 7. This is corrected by substituting for F the tone between F and G, called F-sharp, which changes the interval from 6 to 7 to a step, as it should be, and at the same time makes but a half-step of the interval between 7 and 8.

```
G  A  B  C  D  E  F♯ G
1  2  3  4  5  6  7  8
```

4. The key of G differs, therefore, from the key of C in the substitution of F-sharp for F. The sharp which indicates the new tone is placed at the beginning of the music written in this key, and by it the key is recognized. One sharp placed as here is said to be the sign of the key of G.

5. The tones, then, which form the key of G, are G, A, B, C, D, E, and F-sharp. The scale in G, properly represented, is as follows:

```
G   A   B   C   D   E   F♯  G
1   2   3   4   5   9   7   8
Do  re  mi  fa  sol la  ti  do
```

QUESTIONS.—May any tone be taken as a basis or starting-point for a key? What rule must be observed? What can you say of the representation of the proper order of intervals in the key of C? Is the key any more natural than others? In forming new keys, what method is customary? What tone would this give us for our first new key? Do the intervals come right when G is taken as one? Where do the half-steps occur? Where should they be? How is the difficulty remedied? How does the key of C differ from the key of G? How is the staff fixed to represent the new key? What tones constitute the key of G?

LESSON X.

1. The next key in order is called the key of D, because D is taken as the key-note.

2. To preserve the order of intervals, a new tone is substituted for one of the old ones, as in the key of G, and the following group of tones is the result: D, E, F♯, G, A, B, C♯, constituting the key of D.

3. The sign of the key is two sharps, F♯ and C♯, placed as follows:

4. The pitch names of tones are always the same in all keys, and are therefore called *absolute* names.

5. The numeral and syllable names change with the key, the key-note always being one, and Do. These are called *relative* names, and serve to show the relation of the tones in the key.

SCALE IN THE KEY OF D.

N.B.—It is just as easy to sing in one key as another. Singers must not be troubled about the presence of sharps or flats in a key. If one can sing the scale in the key of C, which has no sharps or flats, he can sing it just as easily in the key of C♯, which has seven sharps in it, and of which the following is the signature:

There is, however, at first a little difficulty in getting familiar with the new place for "one," or Do, but the difficulty is soon overcome, and the change gives a pleasing variety to the study.

The other keys with sharps which are in common use are as follows:

6. *Key of A.* Signature, three sharps (F♯, C♯ and G♯). Tones of the key, A, B, C♯, D, E, F♯, G♯.

SCALE IN THE KEY OF A.

7. *Key of E.* Signature, four sharps (F♯, C♯, G♯ and D♯). Tones of the key, E, F♯, G♯, A, B, C♯, D♯.

SCALE IN THE KEY OF E.

8. *Key of B.* Signature, five sharps (F♯, C♯, G♯, D♯ and A♯). Tones of the key, B, C♯, D♯, E, F♯, G♯, A♯.

SCALE IN THE KEY OF B.

QUESTIONS.—Name the tones which form the key of D. What is its signature? Do the pitch names change with the key? What are the pitch names called? What names do change, as the key changes? What tone is always "one" and "Do"? What do the numeral or syllable names show? Is a key with sharps or flats more difficult to sing in than the key of C? Name the tones which form the key of A. What is its signature? What tone is "one"? What is its syllable name? Name the tones which form the key of E. What is its signature? Where is "do"? Name the tones which form the key of B. What is its signature? Where is "do"?

LESSON XI.

KEYS WITH FLATS.

1. Another method of forming new keys is to take the fourth tone of the preceding scale as the key-note of the new one. The fourth of the key of C is F. A scale beginning with F would appear as follows:

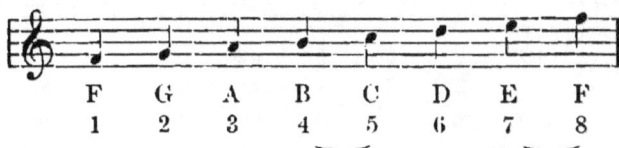

Here, also, the half-steps come in the wrong place; the distance between 3 and 4 is too great and is too small between 4 and 5. By the use of the tone between A and B, called B-flat, (discarding B) the difficulty is overcome, and we have a perfect scale in F, as follows:

2. The tones in the key of F are, therefore, F, G, A, B♭, C, D, E, and the signature one flat.

3. *Key of B-flat.* The fourth of the key of F is B-flat, which becomes the key-note of the next new key.

4. In this key E is dropped and E-flat substituted, giving the tones B♭, C, D, E♭, F, G, A, with two flats, B♭ and E♭, as the signature.

KEY AND SCALE OF B-FLAT.

B♭	C	D	E♭	F	G	A	B♭
1	2	3	4	5	6	7	8
Do	re	mi	fa	sol	la	ti	do

5. Key-notes have tones above and below them; they are considered as "ones" in relation to the tones above them, and "eights" in relation to the tones below them.

6. *Key of E-flat.* In this key A is dropped and A♭ is substituted, making the tones of the key E♭, F, G, A♭, B♭, C, D. Sign of the key, three flats, B♭, E♭, A♭.

KEY AND SCALE OF E-FLAT.

E♭	F	G	A♭	B♭	C	D	E♭
1	2	3	4	5	6	7	8
Do	re	mi	fa	sol	la	ti	do

7. *Key of A-flat.* In this key D is omitted and D♭ substituted, making the tones of the key A♭, B♭, C, D♭, E♭, F, G. Sign of the key, four flats, B♭, E♭, A♭, D♭.

KEY AND SCALE OF A-FLAT.

A♭	B♭	C	D♭	E♭	F	G	A♭
1	2	3	4	5	6	7	8
Do	re	mi	fa	sol	la	ti	do

8. *Key of D-flat.* Tones of the key, D♭, E♭, F, G♭, A♭, B♭, C. Sign of the key, five flats, B♭, E♭, A♭, D♭, G♭.

KEY AND SCALE OF D-FLAT.

D♭	E♭	F	G♭	A♭	B♭	C	D♭
1	2	3	4	5	6	7	8
Do	re	mi	fa	sol	la	ti	do

N.B.—There are other keys, but the preceding ones are all that are in common use.

QUESTIONS.—How are keys formed with flats? What are the tones which make the key of F? What is the sign of the key? Name the tones which make the key of B-flat. What is its signature? When is a key-tone considered as "one" of the key? When is it considered as "eight"? Name the tones which form the key of E-flat? What is its signature? What tones make the key of A-flat? What is its signature? D-flat? Signature? Are there other keys than these?

LESSON XII.

MINOR KEYS.

1. Each major key has a minor key founded upon its tone "six".
2. These keys have the same signature as the major and are therefore called *relative* keys.
3. The intervals of the minor keys are as follows: Half-steps between 2 and 3, 5 and 6, and 7 and 8, and a step and a half between 6 and 7; all others, steps.
4. Tone "six" of the key of C is A. A minor scale founded upon A is represented as follows:

SCALE OF A MINOR.

A	B	C	D	E	F	G♯	A
1	2	3	4	5	6	7	8
Step,	½step,	step,	step,	½step,	step,	½step.	
La	ti	do	re	mi	fa	sol	la

NOTE.—This is called the Harmonic Minor. There are other forms, but this is the proper minor scale and the one in common use.

5. Tone "seven" (in this key it is G♯) is always represented as an accidental and does not appear in the signature place.

QUESTIONS.—How are minor keys formed? Why are they called relative keys? Where do the half-steps occur in the minor keys? What new interval have we in minor keys? Where does it occur? What are the tones which form the key of A minor? How is tone seven always represented? What is the name of this form of minor scale?

LESSON XIII.

EXPRESSIONS. DYNAMICS.

1. A tone that is neither loud nor soft, but medium, is called *Mezzo*; its sign is *m*.
2. A loud tone is called *Forte*; its sign is *f*.
3. A very loud tone is called *Fortissimo*; its sign is *ff*.
4. A soft tone is called *Piano*; its sign is *p*.

176 ELEMENTS OF MUSIC.

5. A very soft tone is called *Pianissimo;* its sign is *pp*.
6. An increasing tone is called *Crescendo;* its sign is *Cres.* or ◁━━━.
7. A diminishing tone is called *Diminuendo;* its sign is *Dim.* or ▷━━━.
8. An increasing and diminishing tone is called a *Swell;* its sign is *sw.* or ◁━━▷.
9. A suddenly diminishing tone is called *Forzando;* its sign is *fz.* or >.

QUESTIONS.—Explain the following terms and give their signs: Mezzo. Forte. Fortissimo. Piano. Pianissimo. Crescendo. Diminuendo. Swell. Forzando.

LESSON IV.

MOVEMENTS.

1. The speed at which a piece of music sounds best, is called its *Movement.*
2. A moderate movement is called *Moderato.*
3. A slow movement is called *Andante.*
4. Between Andante and Moderato is *Andantino.*
5. A fast movement is called *Allegro.*
6. Between Allegro and Moderato is *Allegretto.*
7. A very slow movement is called *Adagio.*
8. A very fast movement is called *Presto.*
8. All these things are in *Rhythmics.*

QUESTIONS.—What is the movement of a piece of music? Explain Moderato. Andante. Andantino. Allegro. Allegretto. Adagio. Presto. In what department is movement?

LESSON XV.

COMPASS.

1. The extend of a person's voice is called its *compass.*
2. Vocal music is usually divided into four parts, called Soprano, Alto, Tenor and Base.
3. Women who sing high tones easily are called *Sopranos* or *Trebles.*
4. Women who sing low tones easily are called *Altos.*
5. Men who sing high tones are called *Tenors.*
6. Men who sing low tones are called *Bases.*
7. Children sing either Soprano or Alto.

VOCAL COMPASS ILLUSTRATED.

N.B.—Since pitches that are an octave apart have the same letter name, it follows that in the whole range of tones there are many Cs, Ds, Fs, etc. To distinguish these names one from another the words "large," "small," "once marked C," "twice marked C," etc., are used. Once marked C is also called "Middle C."

QUESTIONS.—What is meant by compass? What are the common divisions in vocal music? Who sing Soprano? Alto? Tenor? Base? What do children sing? What is the compass of Base voices as shown in the illustration? Tenor? Alto? Soprano? What is the whole vocal compass? How are pitches, having the same letter name but which are in different octaves, indicated?

LESSON XVI.

MISCELLANEOUS.

1. *Modulation* is the passing from one key to another. It may be transient or extended.

2. *Transposition* is the singing, playing or writing of a piece of music in some other key than that in which it was originally composed.

3. A *Slur* is a curved line ⌒ used to connect notes which are to go to one syllable. It also indicates a smooth, connected singing or playing, called *Legato*,

4. A *Tie* is a curved line ⌒ like the slur, but is used only with notes on the same degree of the staff, binding them together, as it were, causing them to represent one continuous tone.

5. *Staccato* means short, detached; its sign is a point.

WRITTEN.

SUNG OR PLAYED.

6. *Marcato* is not quite so short as staccato. Its sign is a dot over or under a note.

7. A *Pause* ⌢ means that the tone may be prolonged at the pleasure of the performer.

8. *Repeat Marks* are dots placed in the spaces of the staff, thus: and show that the music just played or sung is to be repeated.

9. *D. C.*, or *Da Capo*, means that the music is to be played again from the beginning to the close, or to the word *Fine*, which means "end."

10. *D. S.*, or *Dal Segno*, means that the music is to be played again from the sign 𝄋 to the word *Fine*, or the close.

11. *Syncopation* is a change of accent from the usual beat, to that which is generally a weak one.

12. A *Triplet* is a group of three tones played or sung in the time of two. Its sign is a figure 3.

QUESTIONS.—What is modulation? What is transposition? What is a slur? A tie? What is meant by staccato? Marcato? What is a pause? What do repeat marks indicate? What is D. C., or Da Capo? What D. S., or Dal Segno? What does Fine mean? What is syncopation? What is a triplet? What is its sign?

DICTIONARY OF MUSICAL TERMS.

Accelerando; accelerating the time, gradually faster and faster.
Adagio, or *Adasio;* slow.
Ad Libitum; at pleasure.
Allegretto; less quick than Allegro.
Allegro; quick.
Allegro ma non troppo; quick, but not too quick.
Andante; gentle, distinct, and rather slow, yet connected.
Andantino; somewhat slower than Andante.
A Tempo; in time.
Ben Marcato; in a pointed and well-marked manner.
Con Brio, or *Brioso;* with brilliancy, brilliant.
Con Affecto; with expression.
Con Dolcessa; with delicacy.
Con Fuoco; with ardor, fire.
Con Moto; with emotion.
Con Spirito; with spirit, animation.
Diminuendo; gradually diminishing the sound.
Dolce; soft, sweet, tender, delicate.
Doloroso; in a plaintive, mournful style.
Grave; slow and solemn.
Larghetto; slow, but not so slow as Largo.
Largo; slow.
Lento, or *Lentamente;* slow.
Maestoso; majestic, majestically.
Piu; more. *Piu Mosso;* with more motion, faster.
Pizzicato; snapping the violin string with the fingers.
Poco a Poco; by degrees, gradually.
Portamento; the manner of sustaining and conducting the voice from one sound to another.
Presto; quick.
Prestissimo; very quick.
Rallentando, Allentando, or *Slentando;* slower and softer by degrees.
Recitando; a speaking manner of performance.
Rinforzando, Rinf, or *Rinforzo;* suddenly increasing in power.
Ritardando; slackening the time.
Semplice; chaste, simple.
Solfeggio; a vocal exercise.
Sostenuto; sustained.
Tutti; the whole, full chorus.
Vigoroso; bold, energetic.
Vivace; quick and cheerful.

PRACTICAL EXERCISES.

These exercises are designed to accompany the preceding Theory Lessons, and when used in connection with them will be found to form a complete course of elementary instruction in the art of reading and singing by note.

180 PRACTICAL EXERCISES.

9. Five tones.

10. Six tones. Triple measure. Always "beat time."

11. Base staff. All practice reading from this staff.

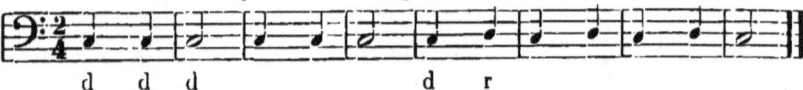

12. What measure? Beats? Rest?

13. What key? What measure?

14. Key of G. What pitch is key-tone. It is just as easy to sing in one key as another.

PRACTICAL EXERCISES. 181

15. Triple measure. Skips.

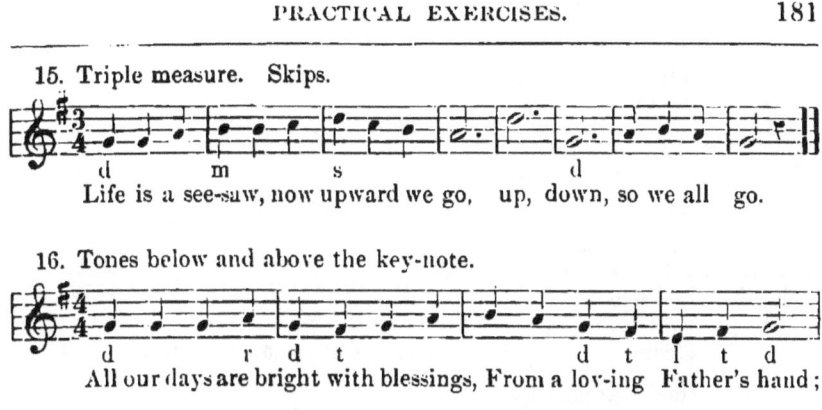

16. Tones below and above the key-note.

17. Base staff.

18. Key of D.

19. Skips. What intervals in the skips?

PRACTICAL EXERCISES.

30. Beginning on Five.

Welcome, sweet day, welcome, sweet day, Drive all the darkness away.

31. All learn to sing from the Base staff.

32. Key of E-flat.

33.

Keep me, Savior, near thy side, Let thy counsel be my guide,

Let thy coun-sel be my guide, my con-stant guide.

34. Make two divisions of the class and sing Nos. 33 and 34 together, after practicing separately.

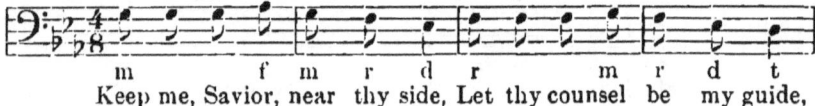

Keep me, Savior, near thy side, Let thy counsel be my guide,

Let thy coun-sel be my guide, my con-stant guide.

35. Key of A-flat.

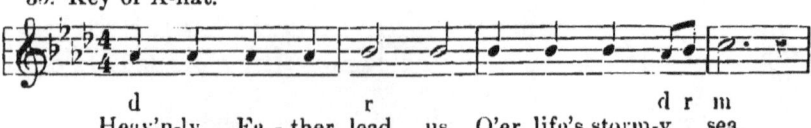

Heav'n-ly Fa-ther, lead us O'er life's storm-y sea,

PRACTICAL EXERCISES.

48. Softly the Shades of Evening Come. With expression.

49. Loving Father.

J. R. M.   J. R. Murray, by per.

1. Lov-ing Fa-ther, hear thy chil-dren Kneeling low be-fore thy throne; O ac-cept our hum-ble wor-ship, Je-sus, Sav-ior, God a-lone. Give us hearts to love thee tru-ly, And to love each oth-er too; Make us gen-tle, kind, o-be-dient, In all things we say or do.

2. Ask-ing not from pain to save us, But from sin, the cause of pain; Cleanse our souls and make us ho-ly, Lead us in thy way a-gain. Give us here thy sweet sup-port-ing, Help us all to do thy will; That at last in heav'nly mansions We may love and serve thee still.

CONTENTS.

Titles in Small Capitals; First lines in Roman letters.

	No.
A glorious day is coming	34
ALL THE WAY HOME	118
ANGEL VOICES EVER SINGING	39
ARE YOU READY	12
ARE YOU COMING	32
ARE YOU ONE OF THE NINETY AND	106
AROUND THE THRONE	8
Around the great white throne	8
As shadows cast by cloud	150
AS THE GROWING OF THE CORN	102
Away all anxious sorrow	145
Away in a manger	148
Backward my heart doth turn	73
BEAUTIFUL LAND ON HIGH	66
Be brave and true	134
BEFORE THE BOLTED DOOR	72
BLESSED ARE THEY	160
Blest be the tie	121
Blessed Savior watch us	137
Brightly beams our Father's mercy	87
Brightly gleams our banner	85
Brothers rally for the conflict	137
CHILDREN'S HOSANNA	23
CHILDHOOD AND THE LILIES	55
CLING TO THE BIBLE	20
CLOSING HYMN	33
CLOSE UP THE RANKS	136
COME, O MIGHTY SAVIOR	24
Come let us all in joyful	156
CONFESSING THE SAVIOR	132
Courage, brother, do not stumble	133
Dear Jesus ever at my side	139
DENNIS	121
DISMISSION	89
Down life's dark vale	84
DO IT NOW	142
ELEMENTS OF MUSIC	161
ENDEAVOR	108
EVERLASTING JOY	76

	No.
Father, draw near to me	65
FALL INTO LINE	114
Five of them were wise	144
FLITTING AWAY	150
FOLLOW THE LIGHT	126
For Christ is our endeavor	109
FOR ME AND FOR THEE	58
FORWARD BE OUR WATCHWORD	81
Forward, Christians	108
FORWARD, MARCH	83
For Sabbath morning bright	141
From the deep star-laden sky	157
Glory be to the Father	127
GLORIOUS DAY	34
GLORIA PATRI	127
GOD'S CARE	73
GOD IS LOVE	69
GO FORTH TO THE FIELD	105
Go forward, Christian soldier	38
GOING TO THE KING	30
GO, PREACH MY GOSPEL	26
Growing together wheat and tares	112
HAIL THIS HAPPY DAY	131
Hail the happy day returning	131
HALLELUJAH, PRAISE THE LORD	96
HAVE YOU NOT A WORD FOR JESUS	18
HELP FOR THE FAITHFUL	57
HELP ME DAY BY DAY	80
HE REMEMBERS ME	115
HIM THAT COMETH TO ME	5
HIS LITTLE ONES	49
HOLINESS BECOMETH THINE HOUSE	61
However small and humble	25
I can not always trace the way	69
If for Jesus you can speak	142
I gave my life for thee	51
In a moment when ye know not	12
In helpless guilt I lay	31
IN HIM	64
I need not go to India	138

(190)

CONTENTS.

Title	No.
IN THE DAYS OF THY YOUTH	46
In the land beyond the shadow	101
In the night when storm	82
In the twilight hours	74
I shall see them and know them	60
IS THEIR ROOM FOR ME	129
I've a guide, tho' the way	71
I will sing of my Redeemer	120
JERUSALEM THE BEAUTIFUL	7
JESUS CHRIST, OUR SAVIOR	100
Jesus thou art the sinner's friend	99
Jesus keep me very near	91
Jesus Savior we will follow thee	86
JEWELS	47
KEEP ME VERY NEAR THEE	91
KIND WORDS CAN NEVER DIE	70
Let your life be one of beauty	76
Lift up your eyes on the fields	27
LITTLE GLEANER'S BAND	41
Lo, he cometh	128
Look up, behold	6
Lord dismiss us	89
LORD THY WORD ABIDETH	187
Lord thy happy children praise thee	141
LOVING FATHER	189
Lord where thy many mansions be	129
LOWER LIGHTS	47
LUTHER'S CRADLE HYMN	148
MAY THY LOVE	87
Mid troubles and dangers	122
MORE THAN ALL	53
MORNING HYMN	116
My light is but a little one	135
MY REDEEMER	120
NEARER TO ME	65
NOW IS THE HARVEST TIME	27
Now to Jesus Christ the glory	35
No voice can sing	77
NOT WORTHY, BUT WILLING	16
Not worthy, O Lord, of thy pardon	16
O BEULAH, LAND OF BEULAH	68
O'er the dreary mountain	45
O HOLY NIGHT	156
Oh lily fair	55
O Lord, our guardian	137
Oh, oft you have heard	4
Oh, sorrowing mortal	9
Oh, the Father's hands are helping	57
Oh, who is the hero	110
O Jesus, gentle Savior	116
O land of princely splendor	92
Once he came	111
ONCE MORE WE GATHER	155
ONWARD ROLL THE AGES	22
O PRAISE THE LORD	158
O Savior help me	80
O Savior, precious Savior	17
O that each day may bring	13
Our anniversary day	152
Our Father, thro' the coming year	117
Our Father who art in heaven	103
OUR RISEN LORD	14
O we are volunteers	62
PRAISE YE THE FATHER	67
PRAYER	119
Purer yet and purer	95
QUIT YOUR FEARS	101
Rest this weary heart	119
REST OF THE WEARY	187
RICH IN MERCY	28
Rise and let him in	72
ROYAL PRAISE	3
See you not the humble widow	53
SHINE ON	135
SING HALLELUJAH	153
Sing them over again to me	97
SING OF JESUS	44
Softly the shades of evening come	188
SOLDIERS, ARISE	59
Soldiers of Christ, march on	10
Soldiers of Christ, arise	59
Some in the ranks are falling	136
SOME THING EACH DAY	13
So will I comfort you	9
SUFFER THE CHILDREN	40
SWING THE GOLDEN CENSERS	140
TEACH ME, O LORD	159
TEMPERANCE	137
TEKEL	146
THAT WHICH WAS LOST	45
THE ANGELS ARE WAITING	124
THE BEAUTIFUL LAND	74
THE CHRISTIAN SOLDIER	38
THE CROSS AND CROWN	123
The cross is for only a day	123
THE GOLDEN CITY	54
THE GOLDEN GATES ARE LIFTED	154
THE HARVEST TIME	6
THE HAPPY LAND	149
THE HOPE OF GLORY	78
THE LIGHT OF THE WORLD IS JESUS	50
THE LIGHT THAT ONCE IN JUDAH	125
THE LITTLE MISSIONARY	138

	No.
The Lord hath need of thee	25
THE LORD IS GRACIOUS	93
THE LORD'S PRAYER	103
The Lord will hold thy hand	31
THE MASTER WANTS WORKERS	48
THE PATHWAY OF LIFE	71
THE PEARLY GATES	151
THE PILGRIMS AND THE PROMISE	92
The Pilot's at the helm	82
THE RIVER OF LIFE	4
THERE'S A LIGHT FROM THE CROSS	37
There's a beautiful land on high	66
There's a city bright and golden	54
There's a crown in heaven for me	58
THERE'S A TABLE OUTSPREAD	75
THERE'S A PROMISE	21
THERE'S A WIDENESS IN GOD'S	143
THERE IS A HAPPY LAND	149
THE SMILE OF THE KING	122
The summer land is just ahead	96
THE SUNDAY BELLS ARE CALLING	11
THE SINNER'S FRIEND	99
THE TEN VIRGINS	144
THE THOUGHT OF JESUS	77
There will come a time	146
The whole world was lost	50
THOU HAST CALLED ME	15
Tho' the storm of life is	63
TIMES OF REFRESHING	98
'Tis a promise sweet to me	5
'TIS BUT LITTLE I CAN DO	113
'Tis not great events	102
TRUST IN GOD AND DO THE RIGHT	133
Trusting in the Lord	63

	No.
Thy word, O Lord	56
WAITING FOR JESUS	130
WAITING FOR ME	60
We are going to the King	30
We are young	88
Weary sinner, hear ye not	32
WE COME, DEAR SAVIOR	42
We come with sweetest anthems	14
We children come, dear Savior	42
WE LEAVE IT ALL TO THEE	117
WE MARCH TO VICTORY	94
We're a little gleaner's band	41
We read of the times of refreshing	98
We stand where Jordan's waves	68
WE WILL FOLLOW THEE	86
WHAT HAST THOU DONE FOR ME	51
What to me are all life's pleasures	78
WHEAT AND TARES	112
WHEN ALL SHALL KNOW THE	43
When he cometh	47
When his salvation bringing	23
WHEN JESUS COMES	84
When Jesus came upon the earth	126
WHEN THE BRIDEGROOM COMES	144
Wheresoe'er my journey	115
WONDERFUL WORDS OF LIFE	97
Work for him gladly	134
WHO IS THE HERO?	110
Yes, his little ones he holdeth	49
YES, WE HAVE A WORD FOR JESUS	52
ZION, BEAUTIFUL BEYOND COMPARE	90

www.ingramcontent.com/pod-product-compliance
Lightning Source LLC
Chambersburg PA
CBHW020844160426
43192CB00007B/779